THE BOOK OF IRISH CURSES

For my daughter
Vera
with a blessing

The Book of Irish Curses

By
Patrick C Power

TEMPLEGATE, PUBLISHERS
Springfield, Illinois 62705

First published in Ireland by
The Mercier Press, Cork

First published in the United States by
Templegate Publishers, Springfield, Illinois 62705

ISBN 87243-060-X

CONTENTS

page

Acknowledgements

I wish to express gratitude to Professor Bo Almqvist of University College, Dublin, for his kindness in allowing me to consult the files of the Department of Folklore in Belfield, Dublin, where the invaluable collection of manuscripts are stored, which contain the only attempt at a systematic sorting and collecting of the old lore of our people. In addition I wish to acknowledge the courtesy and help of Seán Ó Súilleabháin Uas and Captain Kevin Danaher who are attached to that department.

Above all I wish to express my thanks to all the people, some long since deceased, who laboured throughout the years to write out what is contained in the manuscripts. It was a privilege to be able to read what they painstakingly collected and noted in times when so few were aware of the importance of such labour.

Thanks is also due to my good friends Mrs K Hayes, County Librarian in County Waterford, and Miss Fanning of Waterford City Library, who have always seen to it that I was supplied with the books I needed.

I must also thank the anonymous helpers whose lurid curses and picturesque language I have listened to in public houses and private places and have afterwards written down in privacy. They have contributed mightily to this work and are too numerous to be named. Besides, they may not wish such notice, if I know my fellow-countrymen aright.

May I express the wish that the readers of this book never experience personally how effective cursing may be! May they receive only blessings!

Patrick C Power

Chapter I

INTRODUCTION

Some years ago, when John B Keane's play, *Sive,* was first staged in Ireland, audiences were treated to the spectacle of two tinkers appearing on the stage and singing solemnly a ditty which, in part, goes this way:

May the snails devour his corpse,
And the rains do harm worse;
May the devil sweep the hairy creature soon!
He's as greedy as a sow,
As the crows behind the plough—
The black man from the mountain, Shauneen Roo.

Some were startled by this full-blooded curse and others were amused. This was an evocation of the past which could be taken seriously or could be laughed away as mere hocus-pocus and superstition. In the second half of the twentieth century who on earth would ever believe that a curse could be effective? This type of thing must surely be gone away with the oil-lamps and the stage-coaches. That it could ever be seriously held by sophisticated people or urban dwellers that a curse could be placed on anyone was generally regarded as quite impossible and merely superstitious.

Nowadays, however, these matters are due for a serious reconsideration. After all, demonism was also regarded in this light not so long ago but the film, *The Exorcist,* has changed all that to some degree. The old belief that one could bring evil on another by expressing solemnly the wish in words may not be the backward notion that many imagine it to be.

There is a lighter side to this subject. To Irish people the expression 'he was cursing' or 'he was cursing and lighting' means simply the use of picturesque and bawdy language. It always means the use of real cursing terms in a manner less than serious. This aspect of the subject is also rather important and will be noticed in this little work. The use of such earthy and maledictory terms is often amusing, provided one is not the object of the exercise, but it is also regarded as in bad taste and not fit for the ears of ladies and children.

Terms

Since Irish culture is preserved in two languages, Gaelic and English, the material used in this work will draw on material from both. The most interesting facts are generally found in the older tongue, which has been spoken in this country for as long as two thousand years.

The word 'curse' appears to have been borrowed from Gaelic, strange as that may seem. It derives from the word *cúrsachadh*, a word which is no longer found in the language. *Cúrsachadh* meant 'abuse' in the ninth century. It then fell into disuse in Gaelic and found a permanent home in English.

One hears also the word 'malediction' which derives from Latin and means basically to speak evilly. This word is not at all so popular as 'cursing' and has a slightly bookish tang about it when used in everyday speech. The two words enshrine two basic notions about cursing—abusing and evil-speaking.

In Gaelic there are quite a number of words connected with this matter. The most popular is *mallacht*, derived from the same source as malediction. There is also the term *'escaine'* which is as old as written Gaelic. Apparently, it was originally connected with the idea of rendering common or unclean and was used in connection with certain forms of early satirical verse. The form of satire in ancient times known as *glám dícenn* appears to have been a form of cursing as will be shown later on. One might also regard this term as describing a specific form of malediction.

There are also two other words in Gaelic which

should be mentioned. One is *conntracht,* derived from *contradictio* (to speak against), and the other is found in the County Waterford area—*guíodóireacht.* The latter word is also used for 'praying'!

Considering these Gaelic words one notices the ideas of evil-speaking, abusing, rendering common and unclean, speaking against someone, and praying. These give a fairly comprehensive account of what cursing may be all about.

One more interesting word should be mentioned here—the term used by the Irish tinkers. They use *shorknesing,* which may derive from the Gaelic word *seargú* which means withering. If so, one calls to mind the English word so often used in connection with cursing—'blasting'—which has a connotation not far removed from withering.

It is clear from these terms how negative a thing cursing is. Evil is desired for someone in the sense that misfortune and harm may be termed as evil. The use of a word for this practice, which also meant praying, is particularly revealing because the petition of the curser to God is that hurt and evil may fall on another.

It occurs to one that Christianity with its doctrine of 'Love one another' is antipathetic to cursing. Yet the Scripture narrates the tale of Christ failing to find figs on a tree and then withering it with his malediction. As far as the Roman Catholic Church is concerned, one has only to read the decrees of the Council of Trent and notice that after each statement of doctrine the person who refuses to accept it is solemnly declared 'anathema'—cursed. The reader who might be surprised or indeed scandalised at discovering strong use of cursing in a Christian Ireland need not always blame the continuing influence of Pre-Christian practice. There was ample encouragement from Christian ecclesiastical sources for this practice at all times.

Attitudes to Cursing

The general reaction one gets when asking questions

about cursing in the countryside today is: 'Ah! That was done in the long ago! I often heard my mother talking about that kind of thing!' Or else people will say: 'That all went out with the fairies!' The general attitude in modern times is, therefore, that cursing is a thing of the past.

One does find that people fear deep down within themselves that a curse may fall on them, or else, they have never considered the matter because cursing is very seldom used at the present time. When people are stimulated to take an interest in the subject, the frank unbelieving attitude wears away a little and a more primitive outlook may be revealed.

Some surprising facts come to light at times. For example, a Dublin newspaper published the following news item after Christmas 1973:

> Returning a Christmas card from the Minister for Foreign Affairs, Dr FitzGerald, Professor Kennedy Lindsay, a Vanguard member of the Northern Assembly, said: 'I return your seasonal greetings card with contempt. May your hypocritical words choke you and may they choke you early in the New Year, rather than later.' (*Irish Times*, 29 December 1973.)

It should be remarked that Dr FitzGerald is still well in spite of the imprecation uttered by the learned politician from the North of Ireland.

There are some words and phrases which illustrate how much cursing was felt to be an important factor in life long ago in Ireland. For example, a wicked person was described sometimes as *mac mallachtan—* son of a curse. The author also heard a mother, whose family had suffered one misfortune after another, state that 'whoever cursed us, cursed us well!' This echo of old attitudes was also heard some time ago when an old countryman commented on the numerous trials of the family of the late President Kennedy by saying, 'A great curse must have been put on them by someone!'

It appears that Irish people in the past believed that a curse developed a life of its own when pronoun-

12

ced. Colonel Wood Martin in his book, *Traces of the Elder Faiths in Ireland* Volume II, notes that 'a curse must fall on something; if it does not fall on the person on whom it is invoked, it will remain for seven years in the air, ready to alight on the head of the individual who pronounced the malediction.' In Gaelic one hears the saying, which expresses this thought rather gracefully: *Faoi bhun chrainn a thiteas an duilliúr.* ('Under a tree falls its foliage.')

Although the material used in this work is purely from Irish sources, there is one anecdote from the Icelandic sagas worth mentioning. This story, nearly one thousand years old, tells how Gisl, a Viking, was chief among some hostages sent to an Irish chieftain in Connacht. Apparently, Gisl knew Gaelic well and when he met the chieftain, he said, *Male diarik!* — 'curse on you, oh king!' To this far from felicitous greeting the Irishman retorted, *Ogeira ragall!* — 'It's evil to be satirised by a foreigner!' Note how the chieftain regarded the malediction as equivalent to satirising. The Gaelic-speaking Viking expressed his annoyance at his position as hostage in the most telling manner he knew. He must have been all too familiar with the practice already in Ireland.

Reasons for Cursing

The natural reaction of anyone to being wronged or injured is to retaliate with physical violence, or with verbal violence. In a way, this is not necessary in most modern societies because there is redress to be had in the courts of law, or there should be. When all confidence is lost in the judicial system or in the structures of society, there is still the outlet for those who feel wronged by using methods of public protest. Press-campaigns also serve the same end as well as public demonstrations which serve to hold the oppressor up to public odium and force redress to be made.

In societies long ago large sections of the population had very little defence against the rich and powerful. This often led to violence but it was a situation where violence only made matters worse for the down-

trodden. Often the one method left of punishing the wrongdoer was to curse him. The more defenceless the aggrieved person, the more he or she might be expected to use malediction as a weapon to redress grievances.

In the past the most helpless person was possibly the widow. She had no breadwinner, no status, no male protector and the state had little or no interest in its most lowly members. It is not surprising, therefore, that 'the widow's curse' was especially feared in Ireland, as elsewhere. In Southern Ireland there was the saying: 'Shun it as you would a widow's curse!'

Although nowadays and for some time past, the priest in Ireland can hardly be described as downtrodden and helpless, it is true that his curse was especially feared even more than the widow's malediction. This may be due to the fact that he was, so to speak, a professional dealer in the spiritual and could be expected to bring supernatural and supranatural powers into play on his own behalf or on that of others. In the Penal Days the priest was often a fugitive with no rights under the law of the land and this may have been the case also in the first days of Christianity in the country. At all events, the priest's malediction was considered to have a particularly bitter result.

The basic reasons for cursing seem to be frustration in the case of the helpless and the exercise of spiritual powers in the case of priests. Coupled with the priest's curse should be the curse of the poet. In ancient Ireland the poets were an honoured and privileged class in society to an extent enjoyed only by clerics. As a matter of fact, the poets known as *filid* in Pre-Christian Ireland and later seem to have had functions akin to that of seers. In later times, however, the poet's satirical verse was feared but not his curse to the same extent.

Can Cursing be effective?

One hears stories all over Ireland about curses which

15

were put on people and of the subsequent evil which befell them. It is tempting to dismiss all of these as downright lies, or as records of unusual coincidences. This has been the tendency in modern times.

If one dismisses all this lore, how can one deny the truth of what happens in places where voodoo is practised? This may be all primitive magic but if one denies the truth of the effectiveness of cursing, one must then also deny the reality of voodoo. With all its material progress, modern society has not yet explored fully the potentiality of the human mind.

The existence of psychosomatic illness is widely known among medical men and it might amaze people if the true figures of its incidence were obtainable. Is it not reasonable to state that a curse could induce a state of mind which could lead directly to psychosomatic illness and even to death? To admit this is to admit the effectiveness of the placing of maledictions. If one admits the truth of this, one can see that certain conditions may be necessary to make a curse effective. First of all, the victim must be aware that he has been cursed, at least subconsciously. Going even further with this, it can be said that if thought-transference is a reality, then the victim is scarcely immune to his persecutor. Secondly, the curser must believe in his power to bring misfortune on the other and be fully intent on his purpose. If these two conditions are present, it is possible that cursing could be effective.

When one considers how the Irish people in the countryside lived in the past, it can be understood how even the very threat of a curse could have a strong effect. The thousands of parishes were almost self-contained areas with little movement between them. After the Famine in the late 1840s there was large-scale emigration to the United States but little travelling and visiting between the country areas, as in modern days. This provided secure structures of custom but within these areas magical practices, such as cursing, could exercise a power unthinkable nowadays. No secret was inviolable and no mind secure against the assaults which a curser could make.

16

Informal Cursing

Like serious cursing, the use of expletives of a maledictory nature is also a form of verbal violence, ·
although no real harm may be intended. When seen
in print, many expressions in common use seem far
from innocent and yet one hears them quite often.
For example, there is the common 'Damn him!' or
'God blast him!' as well as the lurid 'Hell roast him!'
References to the devil appear in the common expression 'The devil mend him!' and the historically evoca-
tive 'The devil hoist him!' with its reference to
hanging.

All this comes from feelings of temporary annoyance or frustration and it is far preferable to formal
and serious cursing and physical violence. The important distinction between this type of thing and
serious maledictions lies in the intention of the
speaker.

Some informal cursing may have a humorous intention. The 'formula' may be very elaborate and said
with mock seriousness. The most picturesque example
which the author has heard is the following: 'May
the Lamb of God stick his hoof through the floor of
heaven and kick you up in the arse below in hell!' Of
a more rabelaisian kind is the following remark by a
taxi-driver who was describing a journey at speed
over a stony road: 'The stones were hopping off the
car like the curses of Jesus Christ on the windows of
a whore-house!'

Release of frustration, humour, habit, morale-
boosting—all of these may be motivations for the
informal and harmless type of cursing, which is a pale
shadow of the fearful practice which is the ·genuine
thing.

NOTES

The story from the Icelandic sagas mentioned above
is commented on in an article by W. A. Craigie in
Zeitschrift für Celtische Philologie I entitled 'Gaelic
Words and Phrases in the Icelandic Sagas', p. 443.

Craigie suggests *Mallad duit a rig!* for *Male diarik.*
Tomás Ó Moráin B.A. of Clonmel suggested to me
that *Olgeira ragall !* is *Olc aerad ra Gall !* The common
expression which describes someone uttering curse-
expressions—'He was cursing and lighting'—may have
its origin in the belief that one could set a place on
fire with curses, like Jove hurling thunderbolts!

CHAPTER II

TYPES OF CURSES

While the uttering of a curse involved basically only the use of words and a malignant intention, one can distinguish many types of malediction which the ingenuity of people conceived over the centuries. For example, Gaelic distinguishes between *mallacht* (a curse) and *slua-mhallacht*. The latter term means literally a 'crowd-' or 'multitude-curse' and has been translated by Dr P Dinneen in his dictionary as 'a string of curses.' As will be demonstrated further on in this book, it was more than this and was, in fact, the most comprehensive type of curse known to the Irish people. In it all kinds of misfortune were wished on the object of malediction in this life and in the next.

The principal types of curse which one hears of were the hereditary curse, the reverting curse, the group-curse, the cursing contest and the historical curse.

The Hereditary Curse

As the name suggests, the hereditary curse was intended to fall on a person and his descendants. The vicious injustice of this practice needs little comment except to state that it was known to the early Irish saints, apparently, and was counted among the *fácbála* i.e. the legacies of saints whose biographies have been preserved for us.[1] One may, perhaps, see this practice as a reflection of the Christian teaching concerning Adam's sin and the transmission of his guilt and punishment to all mankind. However, if we are to accept as a reflection of historical truth the old legends from Pre-Christian times which Dr Geoffrey Keating includes in his *History of Ireland,* it was known also before this time. He relates that the Ulstermen once forced a queen named Macha to race against steeds when she was in advanced pregnancy. She was victorious but in her premature labour she is said to have cursed the men of Ulster, saying that they would be ill and unfit for service when their country was under attack. The old stories do not narrate more than one incidence of the curse.

A story from County Wexford relates the case of a woman who was keening a relative. During this public lamentation after death it was customary to praise the deceased and also to refer to the circumstances of his death. In this case the dead one had been murdered and the keener laid a curse on the man whom she suspected of the deed. According to this, every member of the family would die without a priest in attendance up to the seventh generation. The recorder of this story mentions that this curse had fallen on the family up to his time—the fourth generation.[2]

In the South of Ireland the most famous hereditary curse is probably that of a widow on the family of the present Marquis of Waterford. This family, named Beresford, took over the land and position of the last Lord Power and Curraghmore after the Williamite War and, although the first Beresford married one of the old family, he and his descendants have always been regarded with distaste by the older families. It is said that one of the Beresfords hanged a widow's only son one day in Seskin, near Carrick-on-Suir, for a trivial reason and that the mother cursed him and his direct descendants for seven generations. The extraordinary fact is that all the owners of the Beresford lands have died violent deaths. This fact can be proved historically and it was noticed in west Waterford generation after generation as war, accident and suicide seemed to prove the genuineness of the malediction. If this be accepted as proof of the power of cursing, the viciousness of its continuation for seven generations is frightening.

In a lighter manner one hears of a family in Maghera, County Tyrone, named McKenna, who are known by the nickname, 'Gorries.' It is said that one

22

of them, Geoffrey McKenna, enlivened the last hours of his life by cursing any of his descendants who took his name, Geoffrey, or 'Gorry.' Apparently, the family heeded the malediction but their neighbours promptly named them 'Gorries' with that slightly malicious humour which is so common in Ireland.[3]

What is one to think of the hereditary curse? If one believes in the power of malediction one accepts it, of course, but if one does not, can it have any validity? Perhaps if someone believes that he is under such a curse, both he and his relatives and neighbours may create the conditions of mind which may bring about its fulfilment. The 'Beresford curse', mentioned above, is notorious and seems to have been believed by many of the family in the past and certainly by all their neighbours. One can only speculate on what effect this can have on the mind of the doomed one. It cannot be idly dismissed as an old wife's tale in such a case.

A Reverting Curse

Like a boomerang, an unjust curse was said to turn back on its originator. The saying 'Curses come home to roost' expresses this idea partially because it was generally held in olden times that any rash use of the deadly weapon reverted on the curser.

An interesting story of a malediction reverting comes from south Tipperary. In Kilmurray parish near Carrick-on-Suir a priest named Father Morrissey died in 1861 after a life which included active church and school-building as well as successfully dispersing an armed group of insurgents in 1848 who had intended attacking Carrick-on-Suir under the leadership of John O'Mahoney, who later built up the Fenian movement in the USA. Seven years before his death Father Morrissey was rather annoyed at the eviction of a parishioner of his. On the Sunday after this event he announced from the altar that he wished that no one would take the land and whoever did, threatened the priest, 'will not die in his bed.' After seven years the land-agent for the area offered the vacant farm to Father Morrissey for a nominal rent and the priest accepted it. In the following autumn he died suddenly in the fields one day and proved the power of his own curse!

Of a different type is the next anecdote. It should be noted that Saint Martin's Eve (10 November) was celebrated in the Irish countryside by the ceremonial killing of a cock and the sprinkling of its blood on the threshold and the four corners of the house. Afterwards the cock was cooked and eaten by the whole household. An old story relates that a house-wife, who was engaged in this Pre-Christian cere-monial on Saint Martin's Eve, laid a curse on the member of the household who first tasted the meat, saying that it would choke him or her. It happened that she was the person who took a portion and she choked to death! This trivial story with its fearful ending may be rationalised by pointing out that per-haps the woman felt a scrap of the food sticking in her throat and then became so hysterical at the thought of her own curse that she choked herself.[4]

The notion behind the reverting curse is worth noticing. One's right to curse is acknowledged but it contains its own punishment for misuse. One gets the impression that this notion was due to some effort to restrain the rash use of cursing.

The Cursing-Contest

As will be apparent later in this book, the cursing-contest was not confined to later Irish history, such as the examples which are given below. It was a feature of maledictory practice in early Christian times, apparently. As the name implies, the cursing-contest was an attempt by two opponents to over-crow one another by strings of maledictions uttered in dialogue form. It is clear to the present writer, at any rate, that these contests were not always seriously intended and they have an element of humour some-times which is rare wherever cursing is mentioned in the old stories and historical or pseudo-historical records.

24

One might begin with a story from County Fermanagh which seems to be typical of the cursing-contest within the last hundred years. It appears that a rate-collector, named Willis, generally expressed his displeasure at the delay in paying the rate-demands by loudly cursing the tenant. One day he called to a farmer, called Murphy, and found that he did not have the ready cash to meet his obligations. Willis began to curse him but Murphy replied in such a fluent fashion that the competitive soul of Willis was aroused. He promised Murphy that if he defeated him in a cursing-contest he would remit the rates and pay them out of his own pocket. If Willis won on the other hand, Murphy promised that he would raise the money somewhere, no matter how humiliating this admission of poverty was. The two commenced cursing and eventually Willis said:

> May your hens take the disorder (the fowl-pest), your cows the crippen (phosphorosis), and your calves the white scour! May yourself go stone-blind so that you will not know your wife from a hay-stack!

To this sally Murphy retorted in the following manner and defeated his opponent:

> May the seven terriers of hell sit on the spool of your breast and bark in at your soul-case! [5]

In this interesting manner the good farmer Murphy secured a total rebate of his rates for the year.

The next example of a cursing-contest is from County Kerry and, while it lacks the humorous undertones of the Fermanagh story, it is hardly to be taken with the seriousness which a venomous curse deserves. The original is in Gaelic. It appears that two fellows, Cod and Pobais, were piking turf one day when Cod awkwardly splashed some turf-mud on Pobais's clothes. The ensuing dialogue then took the following course:

> Pobais: *Léan ort, a mhic an bhrúsaigh, táim salach agat!*
> (Woe to you, you dirty fellow! You've filthied me!)

25

Cod: *Táirnge dearg sa teanga, a dúirt é!*
(A red nail on the tongue that said it!)
Pobais: *Om theanga-sa, go ngaibheadh sé chugat-sa!*
(By my tongue, may it get you!)
Cod: *Íde bricín bheirithe bhrúite ort!*
(The treatment of the boiled broken little fish to you!)
Pobais: *Scoltha an bhradáin siar go cúl ort!*
(The roasting of the salmon to the very end on you!)
Cod: *Le Faill na Saor go dtéir id chrústadh!*
(May you be broken over the Masons' Cliff!)
Pobais: *Ualach sé chapall de chré na h-úir ort!*
(Six horse-loads of graveyard clay on top of you!)[6]

With that parting malediction Pobais ended the contest. It has a bitter tone absent in the preceding example. It should be remarked that the characters, Cod and Pobais, are stock-types in many folklore stories and that this contest mirrors a type of situation well known to the people who enjoyed these stories and for whom they were recited. The mounting bitterness of the curses in the dialogue from insult, through ill-treatment and a cruel death to burial under a mass of earth, should be noted.

In conclusion there is a story heard in the Ballypatrick district near Slievenamon in County Tipperary concerning a cursing-contest between a local man and a tramp which lasted three days. The tramp won the final victory when he said: 'The curse of the goose that lost the quill that wrote the Ten Commandments on you!' If one considers the implications of this curse, its irony will become apparent.

In addition to the usual motives attending maledictory practices, the cursing-contest seems to be a more venomous extension of an exchange of insults between two people. They also illustrate the delight that Irish people take in flowery rhetoric and well-turned expressions.

The Ceremonial Group-Curse
The types of malediction spoken of above involve

one or two people together with the object of the exercise. They also deal with what might be described as private matters as opposed to something which affects an entire community. To deal with an injury which fell on a large number of people something more solemn and serious seemed to be required and this seems to have been the ceremonial group-curse.

The most noteworthy example of this may be what was known as 'The Curse of the Twelve Bridgets' in the Loughrea district in County Galway. It appears that one time a landlord, named O'Hare, evicted a large number of tenants. There seems to have been a large element of injustice in the evictions, as often happened in these times. There was little or no redress in law for the victims and they resorted to male-diction. Twelve girls whose names were 'Bridget' each buried a sheaf of corn on O'Hare's land. They then sat around a quern and took it in turns to rotate it anti-clockwise against the landlord. The results of this elaborate curse are not recorded.[7]

In the Loughrea district also another landlord, named Hardy, evicted a large number of impoverished tenants some years before the Great Famine of the 1840s. To curse him the women made seven straw dolls—the 'Seven Marys'—which they laid out cere-moniously as if they were dead. Then the dolls were 'keened' in the old Irish manner. When all this had been completed, the women took the 'Seven Marys' and buried them on the landlord's ground near his house. It is said that he became bankrupt soon after-wards and left the area.[8]

These curses by women make use of materials which formed part of what was considered 'woman's work' in the long ago. For example, women always bound the sheaves in the cornfields and ground the corn in the quern. They also were the keeners at wakes and cared for the corpses of the dead before burial. The ceremonials described above were, there-fore, particularly feminine. In this case, it was quite appropriate that those most associated with the home—the women—should curse the person who destroyed part of a community by eviction.

28

One further element in the above ceremonial should be noticed—the burial of objects on someone's land so as to bring ill-luck to him. This is not yet extinct in rural Ireland. Nowadays it takes the form of someone putting eggs in the potato-field. In some parts of the South of Ireland this practice has been so prevalent in recent times that priests have felt compelled to condemn it from the pulpit on Sundays.

It should also be remarked that Saint Bridget was honoured in a particular manner by women in the countryside in Ireland long ago. She was, in a sense, the model and exemplar of the woman on the farm, in close touch with beast, hearth and food.

Historical Curses

One of the best-known curses is the 'curse of Cromwell.' The brief sojourn of Oliver Cromwell in Ireland from August 1649 to the early summer of the following year has left deep and abiding memories in the consciousness of the Irish people. Cromwell not only caused death and destruction, as all great military men do, but he also has the great social upheaval of the consequent Plantation associated with his name. To say that the 'curse of Cromwell' was on anyone means in effect that death, destruction and loss of property will come his way. A more whimsical version of the curse of Cromwell is recorded from Tinryland in County Wexford where it meant at one time being subject to rheumatic pains! [9]

In Tinryland also the people of eighty years ago spoke of a curse being on those who supported Charles Stewart Parnell, who fell from leadership of the Irish Nationalists when it was discovered that he was co-respondent in a divorce suit. The curse in this case was rather to the point—it was said that Parnellites would never have sons in their families! [10]

Even to the present day one hears in parts of south Tipperary of the curse on the jury which condemned Fr Nicholas Sheehy to death in the middle of the eighteenth century. Poor Sheehy's case was another example of someone being tried for crimes of which he was not guilty but which were considered by the Protestant ruling class of the times a result of the influence of his type of person. The jurors who voted him to the gallows in Clonmel in 1766 were for ever after, it was said, cursed with physical defects because of their crime and their names are remembered yet among people whose knowledge of Irish history otherwise is scant or barely minimal.

A particular tradition was held in Kanturk in County Cork in bygone times concerning a family of O'Keeffes who oppressed the poverty-stricken people of the area. It was said that when one of this family died, the dogs of the countryside knew it and set up a prolonged barking to mark the event! [11]

NOTES

1. The fácbála is mentioned by Charles Plummer in *Vitae Sanctorum Hiberniae* I, Oxford, 1910. (See Introduction)

2. *Evenings in the Duffrey* by Patrick Kennedy, London, 1875 pp 82-84

3. *Irisleabhar na Gaedhilge* XI p 202

4. *Claidheamh Soluis* III 15 March p 19d

5. Irish Folklore Ms 1403 pp 40-1

6. Folklore Ms 538 p 212

7. Folklore Ms 15 p 220 and Ms 22 p 156

8. Folklore Ms 538 p 456

9. Folklore Ms 407 p 82

10. Folklore Ms 407 p 53

11. Folklore Ms 132 p 126

CHAPTER III

CURSING RITUALS

Cursing was often accompanied by certain rituals, just as religious ceremonies are. The difference between the two, however, lies in the fact that cursing was a personal thing and one does not expect to find a book of rituals for it. The ritual lends solemnity to the act of pronouncing the malediction and provides the drama which man seems to need at moments of great importance.

It appears that pronouncing a malediction from an elevated position was understood to emphasise the pouring down of ill-luck from heaven, as if Jove were hurling thunderbolts in the person of the curser. Even today one hears the expression 'He cursed her from a height!' when someone wishes to imply that someone was foully abused. It seems likely that this old saying embodies an important part of old cursing rituals. An entry in an ancient manuscript from Ireland of the ninth century on the continent would appear to confirm that 'cursing from a height' was known then. An Irish monk glossed the passage which described Shimei cursing David in the valley of Jehosaphet and put the position of the curser on *mullach int slébe*—the summit of the mountain—although the text does not warrant this.[1]

In more modern times the writer, George Moore, in a short story, entitled 'Julia Cahill's Curse', describes a ritual thus:

> a man who was taking some sheep to the fair saw her (Julia Cahill) there. The sun was just getting up and he saw her cursing the village, raising both hands . . . up to the sun, and since that curse was

33

spoken every year a roof has fallen in, sometimes two or three.

This ritual describes the raising of hands and the context, which is not quoted above, describes Julia as standing on a hillock overlooking the village. Were it not for the malediction, one might see this ritual as one for prayerful blessing.

The use of straw for making dolls to curse someone has been noticed in the last chapter. This seems to have been known in connection with a May Day cursing ritual. The lexicographer, Dr Patrick Dinneen, has an interesting note in his Irish-English Dictionary under the word *deatach* (smoke). He tells of a woman cursing a neighbour on May Day as she watches the first smoke arising from the chimney. The woman twists a straw spancel and says: *Im an deataigh úd ar mo chuid bainne-se!* (May the butter of that smoke be upon my milk! i.e. May the butter-fat of these people's cows' milk be upon mine!).

An early play in modern Gaelic refers to a man coming into a farmer's house, laying two blades of grass on the floor in the form of a cross and then cursing the housewife.[2] This rather casual ritual may be paralleled by people in the not too distant past laying maledictions on someone while holding a crucifix in the hand.

The Anvil

The blacksmith was often credited with powers of healing and his forge in the countryside was even more of a meeting-place than the local public house, because women might come to the forge but custom forbade them entry to the tavern in most areas. It is not surprising, therefore, to hear that the anvil was considered to have efficacy when used in cursing rituals, just as water used for dipping red-hot metal was considered to have healing properties.

In the Kiltartan area people believed that a blacksmith turned the anvil as he muttered an imprecation.[3] In north Mayo this power of cursing with the anvil was extended to anyone who had a blacksmith as ancestor. This was quite a chilling inheritance to enter into—the parallel of the hereditary curse.[4]

An example of a blacksmith's descendant turning the anvil is recorded from north Mayo. It is said that a young girl's love-affair with a local boy resulted in pregnancy and that he refused to marry her. As was the custom in these days, she fled to the United States. Her sister, seeing that there was no other redress in the matter, remembered that one of their ancestors had been a blacksmith and she went to a forge and cursed the lover of her sister on the anvil, turning it anti-clockwise. It is confidently asserted that he never had a day's luck from that time onwards.

Cursing Stones

Perhaps the most interesting rituals in maledictory practices were those in which stones were used. Stones, such as gems, are used so often as talismans, that one might expect to have them utilised for cursing and the bringing down of ill-luck.

An old Irish custom, which one hears of, is 'the fire of stones.' A person who wished to curse another, collected a large number of smooth, water-rounded stones and heaped them in the form of a peat-fire. He then knelt in front of the stones and solemnly cursed his victim and invoked ill-luck and misfortune, not only on him, but also on his descendants for many generations to come. The phrase 'until these stones go on fire' was added. Finally, the curser took the stones and hid them singly in inaccessible places with a separate curse on each.[5]

In contrast with the foregoing use of stones, there was the practice of using 'cursing stones.' This strange custom is recorded widely from the west of Ireland and concerned water-rounded stones which were preserved especially for the purpose of malediction. All the available evidence suggests that this custom is very ancient indeed.

One hears of a farmer in west Clare in the last century being prosecuted for beating a beggar-woman. The man said in explanation of his deed that

35

she had threatened to 'turn the stone of Kilmoon' against him. Kilmoon stone was turned anti-clockwise by the curser while the imprecation was uttered and the court-case referred to above is eloquent testimony to what fear the use of the stone aroused in the people. It was said that the Kilmoon stone could turn one's mouth awry.[6]

The noted Irish scholar John O'Donovan speaks of another cursing stone which he saw on the island of Caher, about seven miles north of Renvyle Point in County Galway. This island was much esteemed for sanctity in the time when he was writing and it contains an ancient monastic site and some ruins. The cursing stone rested on the altar of the ruined church there. If anyone felt himself wronged, he betook himself to the island and there fasted and prayed. After these preliminaries, he turned the stone anti-clockwise while uttering a malediction on his enemy. It was believed that then a storm arose, if one were in the right, and the cursed one was destroyed.[7]

Off the coast of Donegal on the island of Tory there was another notorious cursing stone. This particular one could be operated effectively only by one of a family, named Duggan, who had the sole imprecatory rights, apparently. The speciality of the Tory stone was its efficacy in sinking ships. It is said that on one occasion in the last century the cursing stone on Tory was turned against the British warship, *Wasp,* and that it sunk as a result of the malediction.[8]

A much more famous or infamous cursing stone was Leac Cuimín—Cuimín's flagstone—which stood on an old church-site in Kilcummin near the place in Killala where General Humbert landed with his expeditionary force from France in 1798. Nowadays there are two pillar stones north of the ancient church together with an early cross-slab, but formerly there was a cursing stone here too. This differed from others in being flat. It was approximately sixty centimetres long, thirty wide and twenty in thickness.

Saint Cuimín is said to have arrived in this area as an infant and was washed ashore like Moses in a basket. It was said that a man named Maughan found the infant Cuimín and adopted him. In course of time Cuimín showed ecclesiastical leanings and eventually built a little church where the ruins now stand. When he died, it is said, a slab was placed over his grave— Leac Cuimín—and he bequeathed to the Maughan family the power of using this for cursing wrongdoers, and especially slanderers. The Maughan family, apparently, made a livelihood from this stone. If one had a grievance, one fasted for fifteen days, visited the Maughan family and paid a fee for the service to be rendered. Then one walked about Saint Cuimín's Well which was nearby. When all this was completed, the Maughan in charge of malediction, turned the stone against one's enemy.

Leac Cuimín no longer exists today. Sometime before 1840 one Waldron, whose father was Protestant minister in the district, shattered the stone. His father, alarmed at this outrage to local tradition, attempted to bind it together in vain. If young Waldron's object had been to halt maledictory practices, he failed because now each fragment of the stone was considered efficacious in cursing. Eventually the situation grew so serious that Dean Lyons, the administrator of Saint Muredach's cathedral in Ballina, took such fragments of the stone as he could collect and had them built into the walls of the cathedral. There the remains of Leac Cuimín rest today. It is said that one fragment remained for cursing purposes but that is no longer known.[9]

The cursing stones of Killinagh—situated on a parcel of land which juts into Upper Lough Nacnean in County Cavan—are eleven in number and lie in the hollows of a bullaun stone, known as Saint Bridget's Stone. This stone is about one and a half metres long and approximately sixty centimetres in width. It is of quartzite. It is said that Saint Bridget's Stone only had cursing stones in the early nineteenth century but since then two other stones nearby have acquired their own quota. Tradition states that if one turned the stones anti-clockwise and cursed someone, the desired result was obtained if one were in the right. However, it was believed that unjust malediction was never successful when using the stones in Killinagh.[10] One should note that there is an ancient church-site nearby and that it is said that the idol of Pre-Christian Ireland—*Crom Cruach*—once stood here. It may be reasonable to suppose, therefore, that this site may have been the site of both Pre-Christian and early Christian settlements of a religious nature.

The most famous cursing stones of the west of Ireland may be the *clocha breaca*—the speckled stones of Inishmurray. This island is about four miles off the coast of County Sligo and was the site of an early Christian monastic settlement of which many interesting ruins can be seen today. Near the church called *Teampall Mo Laisse* there are five cursing stones which were in use up to at least the Second World War. It is said that a lady went out to Inishmurray to turn the stones against Hitler![11]

Among the other places where cursing stones are found are Trummery Church in County Antrim and Castle Kirk near Lough Corrib in County Galway. It is said that the stones in Castle Kirk—Saint Feichin's Stones—were 'the terror of the land!' In Ballysummaghan in County Sligo there were stones which were turned by members of a family called Summaghan—another example of sole proprietary rights in malediction![12]

It should be noticed that the places where cursing stones were or are found consist mainly of ancient Christian church and monastic sites. One searches in vain for such objects in the ruins of, for example, Cistercian or Augustinian abbeys, which were all founded from the eleventh century onwards. It may be that such practices as the use of cursing stones were part of the type of Christianity which grew in Ireland in the earlier times. It could also have happened, of course, that when the old sites were forsaken by the monks and ecclesiastics after the Reformation that old Pre-Christian practices, which were still strong in the countryside, were carried on in the ruined monastic settlements. The latter view, however, seems unlikely, to say the least of it, and it appears that the use of the cursing stones survived in the early monastic sites as a remnant of Pre-Christian practice. It is an interesting comment on the quality of Irish Christianity and reminds one of the admixture of Christianity and voodoo which is so characteristic of places such as Haiti.

The question which presents itself is why stones came to be used for cursing. This seems to have more than a little to do with the hardness, coldness and lifelessness which seems part of a stone. One hears the saying that someone has a heart of stone—a pitiless heart, in other words. Cursing with such an object would seem appropriate! The offensive use of stones should not be forgotten either. Stones were used in slings and, presumably, were used as hand-thrown missiles in the absence of other weapons.

Colm Cille's Bed

Few of the ancient Irish saints have so many stories of cursing concerning them as Colm Cille, the Irish monk who was born in Donegal in the sixth century and is said to have evangelised Scotland, where so many of Northern Irish folk had settled in that time. One story, which describes a ritual connected with Colm Cille, was called 'sweeping Colm Cille's bed' on someone. This was carried out in the village of Carrickmore, a village about seven miles south of Lifford. The ritual was last heard of in 1866.

Near Carrickmore there is a height which is known as *Mulla na Lap—Mullach na Leapa*—the Summit of the Bed. Here there is a large rock with a crevice, hardly large enough to be described as a cave, about three metres deep and not quite two metres in height. Here, it was believed Colm Cille slept on some occasion.

Whoever wished to curse someone came to Colm Cille's Bed, as the crevice was called, and between sunset and sunrise swept out the floor with a shirt, in the case of a man, or with a chemise, in the case of a woman. The curse was then laid on one's enemy. It was believed that if someone carried out this ritual to curse unjustly, the curse reverted on oneself.[18]

The Glám Dícenn

References to the *glám dícenn* are generally found in poetical tracts and the term is ordinarily understood to mean 'satire' or the like. The exact meaning of the two words need not detain us here. It suffices to say that there is little agreement among scholars on this point. The *glám dícenn* was used by the poets in ancient Ireland and is evidently a survival of Pre-Christian custom.

A reference in a ninth century Gaelic work, under the heading *corrguinecht,* states 'being on one foot and on one hand and one eye making the *glám dícenn,*'[14] From this it appears that while uttering the verse or verses, the poet stood on one foot, raised one hand and closed one eye.

There is another description of the uttering of the *glám dícenn,* which is admittedly rather stylised, but indicates that this was a form of cursing ritual. As one reads it, one feels that this exaggerated ritual may have been insisted on by ecclesiastical authorities to curtail the powers of poets. The cynic may also add that the priests may have preferred to keep the power of malediction within their own bailiwick! Here is this elaborate ritual:

i. The poet fasted on the land of the person whom he wished to curse.

ii. The poet must have received the consent of thirty laymen, thirty bishops and thirty poets before he could utter a *glám dícenn.* (This condition is quite preposterous, of course, but the old Gaelic writers used their imaginations without much restraint!)

iii. With six colleagues the poet went to the summit of a hill at sunrise. To make matters as difficult as possible, it is said that this hill must be where seven 'lands' meet. (Ignoring the second fantastic element here, one should note that the poet was standing on a height, which recalls the belief that one cursed from a height more efficiently than on level ground.)

iv. The poet faced the land of him whom he wished to utter the *glám dícenn* on, while his colleagues faced each of the other six 'lands'.

v. They stood with their backs to a blackthorn.

vi. A north wind must be blowing.

vii. Each of the seven held a stone in his hand and also a thorn. The stone must be a perforated stone.

viii. Eventually, the *glám dícenn* was uttered.[15]

While it is possible that this may be fabrication, there are many elements in the above ritual which find parallels in the rituals already referred to above. Note, for example, the use of a stone and the fasting 'against the person' who is to be injured. As has already been pointed out, the siting of the cursing party on the top of a hillock or rise of ground belongs to cursing practice also. One feels that the fasting, which formed part of many rituals connected with cursing stones, may have been a Christian addition to the business. One finds many examples of such practices in the lives of the early Irish saints. For example, we hear of one Niall who sought sanctuary from Adamnán, the friend of Colm Cille. In spite of this protection, Niall was done to death by one Irgalach. It is recorded that the outraged Adamnán fasted nightly, went without sleep and often plunged himself in water in order 'to destroy Irgalach's life.'[16]

Other Rituals

Other minor rituals are recorded from various parts of Ireland such as one connected with the use of a coin. From the North one hears that in order to curse someone, a sixpenny piece should be taken, bent, and put in a church. With this one used a formula while placing the coin within the church: 'May I bend a coin on the Holy Ghost on you!'[17]

One of the most peculiar rituals, perhaps, is from the Araglin district in County Cork. If one wished to curse a house, one entered it backwards while cleaning a boot! In this case, presumably, the inhabitants of the house would need to be absent when the bearer of malediction was providing such an inviting target to anyone wishing to kick his rear as he entered.[18]

.   .   .   .

Apart from the cursing stones and the elaborate *glám dícenn* ritual, there is little or no homogeneity evident in the various maledictory rituals. The anti-clockwise turning of stones and anvils is a symbol of ill-luck, ultimately connected with sun-worship. Fasting seems to be connected with Christian practice, although this need not be so.

If one were to attempt to describe what may have been a 'basic' ritual, one might possibly say that the curser stood on a significant site, such as a height overlooking his victim or his victim's property, or else went to some place of religious importance and there pronounced his malediction.

One hears of cursers laying hold of varied objects, such as crucifixes, when laying maledictions. This was always spontaneous. One feels that the use of such objects, as well as the handling of cursing stones, symbolised the mental and spiritual violence which was intended instead of the purely physical.

Cursing rituals were, therefore, symbolic and extremely varied. They added drama to the act of will and increased the emotional impact on the curser and, as one is inclined to believe, added efficacy to the malediction.

NOTES

1. *Thesaurus Paleohibernicus I* Cambridge, 1903, Strachan and Bergin 58c 4

2. See *Claidheamh Soluis* VIII 23 pp 4/5 1906

3. Folklore Ms 433 p 203

4. Folklore Ms 1340 p 380 Story immediately following this is from same ms pp 89-91

5. *Elder Faiths of Ireland* Vol II Col. Wood-Martin p 58 London, 1902

6. *Journal of the Royal Society of Antiquaries of Ireland,* Vol XXX p 306, 1901

7. *Journal of the Royal Society of Antiquaries of Ireland,* Vol XXX p 357, 1901

8. *Irish Press* article by Seamus Ó Néill 17 Nov 1967—'Curses of Ancient Stones'

9. Folklore Ms 109 p 110

10. See *Shell Guide to Ireland* London 1962 (Killanin and Duignan), under *Blacklion*

11. *Journal of the Royal Society of Antiquaries of Ireland,* Vol XXX p 357

12. *Journal of the Royal Society of Antiquaries of Ireland,* Vol XXX p 357

13. Folklore Ms 102 p 60

14. *Three Irish Glossaries* London 1862 Whitley Stokes p 63

15. See *Irish Classical Poetry,* Dublin 1960 pp 76-77 Eleanor Knott

16. *Silva Gadelica* London 1892 p 407 Standish H O'Grady

17. *Béaloideas IV* p 20

18. Folklore Ms 54 p 361

Chapter IV

THE SAINT'S CURSE

In spite of the critical remarks against cursing usually delivered by Christian moralists, it was nothing unusual among those considered to be models of Christian living—the saints. Indeed Christ is seen in the Gospel as cursing a fig-tree which he found unfruitful and it withered as a result. Further back one finds the 'Cursing Psalms' which, as a rural wit once expressed it, 'would raise the paint off a door', so violent are they!

The hagiographers who passed on to us the accounts which we possess of the early Irish saints (circa A.D. 450 to 800) endowed their heroes with fearful powers of cursing. It may be suggested that all this was pure fiction, written down to give the saintly people added status in the eyes of their fellow-Irishmen. If this were so, one must agree that the readers of the hagiographies were familiar with cursing and it is also possible that the early Irish saints also practised malediction in some cases. One just cannot dismiss the frequent mention of the saint's curse as being completely without historical foundation of any kind.

It is instructive at this time to recall the siting of the cursing stones in so many early Christian monastic sites. The accomplished cursers of the hagiographies may have found a thriving home-grown custom to practise and not some notion which came from abroad.

Saint Patrick

It is sometimes a source of wonder to readers of the life of the alleged Apostle of Ireland—Patrick—how radically different his personality is in the short autobiographical *Confessio* from that found in the *Tri-*

47

partite Life of Saint Patrick, written nearly four centuries later. In the intervening time, the humble harassed missionary has become a wonder-worker and a hurler of maledictions on anyone who impeded his triumphal journey through Ireland. It is worthwhile taking a look at the cursing clerical bully of the later work.[1]

The total number of maledictions mentioned in the later work are about thirty. They vary from a curse placed upon an area where inferior yew-wood grew —wood unfit to repair the saint's chariot—to a malediction placed on a tyrant who had ill-treated his slaves and refused to heed Patrick's entreaties on their behalf.

The story about the cruel slave-owner is as follows: Patrick approaches a group of slaves who are felling a yew-tree. Their hands are bleeding profusely because, they explain to him, they had been forbidden to sharpen their tools sufficiently. This, by the way, may reflect something which came to the notice of the hagiographer in the late ninth century. Patrick went at once to the dwelling of the slave-owner who refused him a hearing. To bring him to heel, the saint fasted against him at the entrance to his residential site. When this proved unavailing, Patrick next spat on a stone and the spittle penetrated it. Then the saint cursed the stubborn slave-owner and said that his family would never produce a king or the heir to a king. To round off this story, the writer informs us that the stubborn man who had resisted the saint was drowned in a lake soon afterwards.[2] Notice the part that fasting and a stone play in this story.

Some of the curses are monstrously frivolous. The saint comes to Inbhir Domnand, for example and finds no fish there. We are told simply that he utters a curse on it and that it lacks fish ever since then.[3] The Hill of Usnagh, hallowed in Pre-Christian Ireland, also suffers malediction when Patrick and his fellow-missionary, Sechnall, collaborate in cursing the stones there:

'Maldacht', ol Patraic ('A curse!' said Patrick)

'for clocha Uisnigh', ol Sechnall ('On the stones of
Usnagh', said Sechnall)
*'Bith dano', ol Patraic, 'ní dénaither cid clocha
fotraichi díb!'* ('So be it, indeed', said Patrick,. 'Of
them not even heating stones will be made!')[4]

It should be explained that heating stones were used
to bring up the temperature of water for bathing in
these times.

Personal violence to Patrick or his friends was also
the reasons for malediction. A certain family-group
were unlucky to stone Patrick and his people and they
earned the following curse:

*Mo débrod . . . no comlund i mbethi memais foraib
ocus bethi for seilib agus for sopaib hi cach airiucht
i mbed!* (My sorrow . . . you will be defeated in
every engagement you take part in and in every
assembly you attend you will be spat on and
reviled!)[5]

Some misguided wretch used a psalm-book as missile
with which he struck Patrick. On this fellow, the pious
hagiographer tells us, Patrick put a curse which led to
the loss of a hand later.[6] And then one reads of the
members of a family who whipped the servants of the
saint. The curse inflicted on these people was that
they would be barren henceforth.[7] One gathers the
opinion while reading the *Tripartite Life* that one did
not touch or injure with impunity the good saint or
his servants and friends.

There is one anecdote which concerns 'pagans'
specifically. It happened, we are told, that these people
were digging a *ráth*—an earthwork around a domestic
settlement—on a Sunday. For this breach of Christian
sabbatarian laws Patrick uttered a curse against them.
The result of this malediction was that a great storm
arose which swept away the results of their labours![8]

One interesting story is related which concerns a
curse which was eased. It is related that Patrick's
horses were taken by the people in an area and, of
course, the good saint rained down curses on them.
However, luckily for them, they had a bishop who

49

interceded on their behalf and the curse was eased. Then the story goes on: . . . *ro nig Máine cossa Pátraic cona folt ocus cona déraib ocus ro immaig na echu i fergorrt ocus glan a cossa ar honóir Pátraic.* ('. . . Máine, the bishop, washed Patrick's feet with his hair and his tears and he set the horses on grazing-ground and washed their feet in honour of Patrick.')[9]

These anecdotes from the *Tripartite Life of Saint Patrick* may be seen as reflections of Irish life in the ninth century as seen from a monastery. Evidently it was understood that a great saint should be not only a great worker of miracles, but also a fulminator of curses on all who hurt or thwarted him or his followers. The biographer attempts to show the saint as equal to or even greater than the pagan heroes whose fame was in the mouths of the storytellers. The thought also occurs to one that the writer may have known of ecclesiastics in his own time who laid maledictions on their enemies and he surely heard plenty of stories of what happened or was alleged to have taken place in the past.

Saint Colm Cille

If Patrick be considered the patron saint of Ireland, Columba or Colm Cille, as he is known in Gaelic records, was honoured as secondary patron saint of Ireland. Much legend has gathered around his name and he is described as cursing people from time to time. Already the cursing ritual, known as 'Sweeping Colm Cille's Bed' against someone, has been mentioned.

While Patrick was a foreigner, Colm Cille was an Irishman who is said to have mediated between the poets and their enemies at the Convention of Druim Ceat in County Derry in A.D. 575. It is said that he was accused by the wife of the king who convened this meeting of *corrguinecht*, a term which has been referred to already as some type of ritual connected with uttering the *glám dícenn*.

Many 'homely' curses survive in folklore of interest on the subject of malediction. One hears of Colm Cille

50

cursing someone who roasted a herring with its belly to the fire-embers! This story comes from County Donegal where the saint was born.[10] From the same area we hear that once the good man was crossing a weir and slipped from it into the water. He then is said to have laid a curse on that place and said that herring would never come up the river to this place until a bridge was built there. We are solemnly assured that the curse was effective until the waterway was bridged at this point.[11]

A rather peculiar story is recorded from Kells in County Meath where Colm Cille is reputed to have founded a monastery. It is said that he laid a malediction on a family, named Haughey, saying that they would remain there for ever! [12]

Of a more domestic nature is the curse which Colm Cille is alleged to have laid upon housewives who did not turn both sides of the cake to the fire when cooking the griddle-bread long ago.[13]

The last story forms part of a series which describes a journey made by Colm Cille in County Tyrone. As he went on his way he distributed maledictions as he went. In a place called Stráid the children threw clods and stones at the holy man, unchecked by their parents. He was informed that the adults were attending a large number of weddings from the area that day and their children were amusing themselves. At this he burst into malediction: 'My curse on Stráid,' said he,. 'May there never be more than one couple from one townland married there! '[14]

He then reached Crossconnell and met a man standing on the roadway. Their little conversation went as follows:

'Will this road bring me to Leenan?' asked Colm Cille.
'I don't know whether it will or not!' answered the man.
'My curse on you and Crossconnell,' retorted the irate Colm Cille, 'and may it never be without a fool!'[15]

After this malediction the good man proceeded further

and found himself in Eightercloona. Feeling the need for some nourishment, he asked a woman for a piece of bread. The lady did indeed have bread but it had broken after the baking and fallen into the red ashes. The misfortunate housewife then heard Colm Cille curse her townland, saying that it would never be without red ashes.[16]

The last lap of this maledictory journey was reached when Colm Cille reached a place which was known as Ballinamallaght (*Baile na Mallacht*—Townland of the Curses) near Plum Bridge. At this stage of his journey he desired to know the time of day but there were no cocks in the area whose crowing might indicate what time it was. Predictably, he cursed that place also, saying that there would be no more cocks there ever again.[17]

Finally one should refer to what is known often as 'the curse of Colm Cille' par excellence: *Leisce chun luí agus leisce chun éirí*. (Reluctance to retire to bed and reluctance to arise.) This is said to have been the saint's curse on his fellow-Irishmen—their hereditary curse which is derived from Colm Cille.

The Cursing of Tara

Of all the curses said to have been uttered by saints, the malediction on Tara is probably the most famous one. It grew around the king, Diarmuid, who died in battle in A.D. 558 and is said to have been the last king to have lived on the hill of Tara in County Meath.

The story begins with the sending of an agent by the king, Diarmuid, to one Aed Guaire of the territory of Uí Máine, an area comprising parts of the present Counties of Clare and Galway near the river Shannon. The agent arrived at Aed's residence in the owner's absence and insisted that he be admitted holding his spear horizontally. To enable him to do this, the doorway was widened and then he entered. When Aed returned and saw the destruction done to the doorway of his house, he slew the royal agent without ascertaining in time who he was. When he discovered his error,

Aed fled to Muskerry in County Cork to a bishop who was related to him. This proved no protection to the hot-tempered Aed and he decided to seek sanctuary with Ruadhán of Lorrha in the present County Tipperary. Diarmuid pursued him here also and the fugitive was forced to go to 'Britannia'—probably Wales, where there was an Irish colony. So influential was Diarmuid, however, that Aed had to flee from here back to Ireland and Ruadhán offered him a hiding place in Ossory named *Poll Ruadháin* (literally 'Ruadhan's cave or hole'). This may be Polerone in County Kilkenny or another place of similar name near Kilmoganny in the same county. Here at last Diarmuid found him and murdered him.

Ruadhán now took action. Diarmuid had made the mistake of offending one who has been described specifically as he 'who loved cursing'. This description occurs in a poem specifying the principal virtue of each of the major early Irish saints. Ruadhán took his friend, Brendan of Birr, with him and appeared before Diarmuid's residence on the hill of Tara. First the two monks rang their bells against the king and then fasted against him. First fruits of these preliminaries were that twelve hostages in Diarmuid's care died. This did not overawe the tough Diarmuid in the least, who forthwith fasted and prayed against the two clerics. Evidently, Ruadhán and Brendan felt they were dealing with formidable opposition in their own field, so they decided to trick Diarmuid into breaking his fast. They pretended to be eating and when the king saw this from afar, he was deceived and took some food. When Diarmuid realised that he had been tricked, he began to curse Ruadhán and the saint replied in kind. This cursing contest is the oldest one extant in Gaelic literature. Here is how it goes:

Diarmuid: For what you've done, Ruadhán, you'll be requited by the Blessed Trinity, because your monastic family will be the first to decline in Ireland.

Ruadhán: Your kingdom will decline first and none of your descendants will ever reign.

Diarmuid: Your beloved place will be deserted. . .

Ruadhán: This royal city of yours will be empty within a hundred years. . . .

And thus it happened that the leader of the cursing saints found himself dealing with a worthy protagonist who bandied malediction with him as an equal. It is noticed by the annalists that Diarmuid was killed in Ulster fighting the Dál n-Áraide and that Tara was abandoned afterwards as an habitation site.[18]

This interesting story of confrontation is unique in showing us a king and an ecclesiastic both competing on equal terms in a cursing contest. It symbolises (if it does not actually also report the factual truth) a struggle for the right of giving sanctuary or refusing it. In the stories of Saints Patrick and Colm Cille the cursers are omnipotent and unopposed in their maledictory practices, while it is quite otherwise here. This story has the ring of historical truth.

The ritual used comprises fasting and bell-ringing and then the utterance of formulae. Indeed the actions of Brendan and Ruadhán seem very like a form of excommunication, which is, of course, the official cursing ritual of the Christian Church. Apart from the death of the twelve hostages, which has the smack of voodoo about it, Diarmuid's death in battle was not extraordinary for an Irish king for these times. A glance at the annals for the period A.D. 500-800 will readily prove that very few kings and chiefs died peacefully. Therefore, Ruadhán could confidently curse Diarmuid with death in battle; it was an occupational hazard. The dereliction of Tara is quite another matter and this was the chief malediction, followed by the reference to none of Diarmuid's people ever again being king.

The Madness of Sweeney

One of the stories beloved of Gaelic scholars now and in the past is *Buile Shuibhne*—Sweeney's Madness. Sweeney was king of the Ulster people, named Dál n-Áraide, at whose hands Diarmuid of Tara died in battle. The story is centred round an historical event—

55

the Battle of Moira, which took place in A.D. 637. In this battle the Dál n-Áraide were defeated but their king, Sweeney, survived the slaughter and spent the rest of his days as a lunatic in the woods of Ireland. It is said that this was the result of a saint's curse before the battle.

At the centre of the story with Sweeney was Rónán, the abbot of Drumiskin in the present County Louth. Rónán's first confrontation with Sweeney happened when Sweeney took by force from him a multi-coloured tunic which was to be presented to another. For this the saints of Ireland cursed Sweeney.[19]

Before the Battle of Moira Sweeney heard one day the ringing of a bell and asked his people who was the ringer. When he heard that it was Rónán, he became enraged and decided to expel the cleric. His wife endeavoured to restrain him and laid hold of his cloak but he burst away from her, leaving the garment in her hand and appeared 'naked', as the old story expresses it, before Rónán. Rónán was singing his psalms contentedly out of his psalter when Sweeney snatched the book from him and threw it into a lake nearby. He then laid hold of Rónán by the hand and began to drag him away, but news of impending battle arrived and spared Rónán further molestation.

Rónán recovered his psalter that night when an otter very obligingly fetched it from the water for him! He then thanked God and got along with the serious business of cursing Sweeney. Here is the formula he used:

> By the permission of the powerful Creator, which I have: Just as he came to expel me when he was naked, may he always be flying and straying naked throughout the world until death at spear-point takes him. My curse ever upon Sweeney and my blessing on Eorainn (his wife) who tried to hold him. . . .

This was the second curse on the luckless Sweeney.

In spite of what had happened, Rónán endeavoured to prevent the Battle of Moira when the two armies had assembled, but all his efforts were frustrated by

Sweeney, who seemed bent on his own destruction. Finally, before the battle Rónán and eight of his monks blessed Sweeney's allies by sprinkling them with holy water. When it came to Sweeney's turn, he was sprinkled in such a manner that he thought he was being mocked and he killed one of the monks with his spear. He attacked another one but hit the little bell which the man carried on his breast, and the shaft of the spear went high in the air. The bell-owner then pronounced a third curse on the hot-tempered fellow:

I pray the powerful Creator that you may go as high as the shaft of the missile and in the clouds of heaven as any bird and may the death you gave my companion—death at spear point—come also on you.

Sweeney and his allies were defeated in the battle which followed but the king became a lunatic. He lost, not only his kingdom, but also his wife who re-married. The mad king lived ever afterwards in the woods of Ireland nesting on the trees and shunning society. The storytellers relate that one day he approached a woman to ask for food and that her husband came on him talking to her. Without investigating any further he killed Sweeney with his spear, thinking that he was about to be cuckolded. The last part of the curses was thus fulfilled.[20]

This story appears to be a rationalisation of the fall of the Dál n-Áraide people from the point of view of a society which could not account for the eclipse of an ancient and vigorous race. The curse pronounced by Rónán and that uttered by his clerical companion are preceded on one hand by a request for permission to curse to God and on the other hand by a direct prayer. It all seems to be part of the protective barrier raised about themselves by the clerics against the violence of their fellow-countrymen that such stories of effective cursing should be known and believed.

The Curse of Maedoc

'Maedoc' is the Latin version of the name of Maodhóg,

which is generally anglicised 'Mogue'. It means simply 'My young Aed', a reflection of discipleship, a common practice among the early Irish saints where one finds a name such as Mochuda—'My Cuda'.

It is said that some relatives of Maedoc were taken captive by a raiding party and brought to the district of Ui Chonaill Gabhra, which roughly corresponds to part of modern west Limerick County. When Maedoc heard of what happened, he went to the raider-chief's house and demanded the release of the captives. He was refused and told to leave the house. He then spent three days outside the dwelling fasting against the chief. At the end of the fast the chief's daughter died but Maedoc raised her to life at the request of her mother. In spite of this, the chief was not impressed and then Maedoc proceeded to curse him solemnly. As he began, a youngster who was standing nearby asked him to transfer the curse to a large boulder. When this was done, we are told, the boulder split in two! This had the desired effect and the chief released the captives. In the form of bonus, Maedoc also secured the site for a monastery in the area![21]

This story resembles slightly the one concerning Saint Patrick defending the ill-treated slaves, which has been quoted above. In both cases the motive was humanitarian and, one might add, worthy of a saint's maledictory powers.

Maignenn

Maignenn was the ancient Irish saint who gave his name to Kilmainham (*Cill Maignenn*—Maignenn's Church) near Dublin. There are some interesting stories about him, where cursing is concerned.

First of all, one hears that he visited a grave where a pagan was buried and called on the spirit of the deceased to speak to him and those who were standing around. The spirit stated that he had terrorised the strong and robbed the weak as well as wronging churches. He then concluded with the statement that this resulted in his receiving 'the crying of bells and extinguishing of candles and the curses of the faithful,

58

so that he died unrepentant of his sins'.[22] This is a clear reference to both excommunication and what one might call 'lay cursing'.

There is then another story concerning a thief who stole the only cow belonging to a female leper in Kilmainham. She went for redress to Maignenn and his company of clerics. They were so enraged by her complaint, that they rang their bells and poured forth curses and abuse on the thief. After this outpouring of malediction in unison they noticed that Maignenn remained silent without stirring hand or foot. He broke his silence eventually to state sympathetically that he should have to bestow his blessing on the thief, because there was no one among the faithful who would give him either his wish or even a sign, because he was doomed to hell where no one could help him![23]

The hagiographer who wrote Maignenn's life relates that Maignenn would act as judge by Patrick's side on the Last Day over those monks who obeyed the saint's injunctions or rule. As for those misfortunates who did not, both Maignenn and his friend, Maolruan of Tallaght, cursed them to a death by sharp weapons and an eternal sojourn in hell with the three most merciless devils, who are, we are told, Beelsebub, Mailmantas and Sailemas! A most elegant conclusion to their terms of life! Here again is the invocation of cursing to strengthen the hand of the ecclesiastic.[24]

Varia

There is a story recorded from County Fermanagh to account for the fact that a particular river has few if any fish. It is said that Saint Feber was one day crossing the river by a ford and the holy man's books were carried across on the back of a deer. The animal slipped in the river and spilled the books into the water. As a result of this accident, we are told, Feber cursed the river that it would be without fish henceforth. This story has more than a touch of nature-worship in the idea that the river could harm someone consciously and be punished for the fact![25]

59

Of a more unconsciously humorous type is the story from Kanturk in County Cork concerning a female saint. This good lady was passing by a forge carrying coals in her lap. The blacksmith admired her shapely ankles so much that, we are informed, she sinned and set the coals on fire! She then laid a curse on him and any other smith who ever lived in the area afterwards saying that they would never be able to weld iron by hand! [26]

A curse laid on tradesmen is also recorded from Ring, near Dungarvan in County Waterford. Stonemasons long ago in this region were notorious for their broken boots and they also were forced by the nature of their work to travel far and wide for employment. It is said that Saint Patrick once met three masons and gave them a shilling and a groat each to relieve their poverty. Instead of using this sensibly, the three fellows spent it all on drinks. Patrick heard of what they did and we are told that he put a malediction on them that they and all stone-masons would have a long walk and broken boots for ever.[27]

And then finally there is this story of a saint averting a curse. The tale originated in Kilmacduagh in County Clare. One morning a poet met a saint at the church door and said: 'May there be a corpse here every Monday morning!' The saint did not relish this and so he retorted: 'If so, may it be a starling's! '[28]

. . . .

The theory of Charles Plummer that the inclusion of curses in the lives of the early Irish saints was to increase their stature is partly true but it is hardly the full reason for the part played by maledictions in the stories. It surely was sufficient to portray the wonder-working powers of the saintly hero without ever resorting to cursing of any kind.

It appears that an important reason was that the writers of these lives were familiar with maledictory practices in connection with monasteries. One remembers the siting of the cursing stones and this was hardly fortuitous. One is inclined to assert that the

60

cursing stories were not all fabrications but that many of them were based on fact. After all, if a saintly man could work good with miracles and was believed to be capable of it, what would be easier for him and his friends to believe but that he could bring evil with malediction to punish his enemies and the enemies of the community whose good he had at heart?

Many of the curses of the saints could be described as excommunication rites. This was the use of the Christian Church and is still available to the authorities of the Roman Catholic Church. The ringing of bells and the custom of fasting beforehand against the person to be cursed belong to this rite. Of course, bell-ringing is not specifically Christian but is part of the noise-magic which endeavours to scare away evil spirits according to the old saying: 'The more din, the more luck.' Fasting could also be described as derived from magical customs which are Pre-Christian. It was really both an act of self-purification and a pressuring of the person whom one wished to curse.

The above thoughts occur to one when reading the lives of the early Irish saints. In the case of folklore stories one finds a different type of tale. The literary tales describe a ritual but the popular stories speak of the circumstances of the malediction and supply the formula. They also have the appearance of being part of an almost casual growth, while the literary types are either careful fabrications, imitations of other tales or else are partly true stories. All the most justifiable scepticism in the world about this type of thing should not blind one to the fact that many of the stories found in the hagiographies may be based on fact. Where the purely folklore tales are concerned, one is justified in being extremely sceptical where saints' curses are concerned.

NOTES

1. *Bethu Pátraic*, Dublin, 1939, edited by Kathleen Mulchrone. This is the *Tripartite Life of Saint Patrick*
2. op cit p 130

3. op cit p 23
4. op cit p 51
5. op cit p 85
6. op cit p 97
7. op cit p 45
8. op cit p 134
9. op cit p 88
10. *Béaloideas* Vol III p 49 (Seamus Ó hEochadha)
11. *Béaloideas* Vol III p 49 (Seamus Ó hEochadha) p 55
12. *Ordnance Survey Letters* (John O'Donovan) *County Meath,* 1936
13. *Iris na Gaedhilge* Vol X p 565
14. *Béaloidea*s Vol II 1930 p 359 Éamonn Ó Tuathail
15. *Béaloideas* Vol II 1930 p 359
16. *Béaloideas* Vol II 1930 p 360
17. *Béaloideas* Vol II 1930 p 361
18. *Vita Sanctorum Hiberniae* by Charles Plummer, Oxford, 1910, pp 246-247
19. *Banquet of Dún na nGedh* ed by John O'Donovan p 39
20. *Buile Shuibhne* ed by J G O'Keeffe, Dublin,1952, pp 1-6
21. *Acta Sanctorum Hiberniae,* John Colgan, Louvain, 1645, p 212
22. *Silva Gadelica* ed by Standish H O'Grady, London, 1892. See *Betha Mhaignenn* pp 37-48
23. See *Betha Mhaignenn* pp 37-48
24. See *Betha Mhaignenn* pp 37-48
25. *Ordnance Survey Letters* (John O'Donovan) *County Fermanagh,* 1834
26. Folklore Ms 132 p 132
27. *The Irish of Ring* by Risteard B Breathnach, Dublin, 1947, p 115
28. *Béaloideas* Vol VI p 60 by Seamus Ó Duilearga

CHAPTER V

THE PRIEST'S CURSE

In a way the saint's curse may be seen extended in the curse which a priest was thought to be capable of putting on a person. It may be difficult nowadays to realise that this was done in the past and it was feared very much indeed. The great powers which the priest was understood to wield explain this to some degree and it must also be remembered that in country areas especially the influence and power of the priest were enormous. It should not be forgotten either that the superstitious and credulous people who formed the flock of the typical parish in the countryside in bygone days often saw malediction where none had been intended. Even in 1961, when a parish priest spoke out in anger during a sermon against those who had not subscribed to a church collection and ended with the words, 'These people may yet be without money themselves', some folk were very disturbed and asked, 'Is he trying to curse us?' Another priest in these times preached in a village church about the evils wrought by anonymous letter-writers. Eventually he revealed that someone had complained of him to the bishop in this fashion and ended his sermon solemnly, 'May the hand wither off the person who wrote that letter about me!'

The priest's curse may be a thing of the past in most of Ireland, but the above examples illustrate that the attitude which may have encouraged it in the past is not quite dead everywhere yet and neither is the actual curse itself.

The Curse of the Clanna Buí

Sleady Castle near Modeligo in County Waterford was the home of a family named the MacGraths. It was

65

built in the early seventeenth century. Although the head of the family during the Post-Cromwellian period did not actually have to leave his home, the family in general lost their power in west Waterford. Nevertheless members of the MacGraths settled in the hilly area of Tooraneena between Dungarvan and Clonmel where they exerted great influence among the people who feared them. These MacGraths became known as the *Clanna Buí*—the yellow family, not because they lacked physical courage, but due to the sallowness of their skin.

The *Clanna Buí* were both feared and hated in the area where they first lived in the early eighteenth century. They operated as tithe proctors for the Protestant clergy and generally ingratiated themselves with the authorities. As for their reputation among the local people they were regarded as *braobairí bora gan truagh gan taise*—'rough tear-aways without pity or softness', as an old account states.[1] Although they remained Roman Catholics, the *Clanna Buí* were not very friendly with the priests, to put it mildly, until one of the family became a priest in the beginning of the nineteenth century and then the situation changed radically.

Sometime towards the middle of the eighteenth century two men of this family had a disagreement on some business matter and they met in the village of Tooraneena to discuss it. The two locked themselves in a room of a house, which can still be seen, and went from discussion to acrimonious dialogue and from this to fighting. So fierce was the fight that one killed the other. So great was the influence of the family with the authorities that the survivor was not put on trial for his life, as he should have been. However, the local priest decided to do something about the matter. On the Sunday following the killing, the priest condemned MacGrath publicly from the altar in Tooraneena and finished his statement with a *slua-mhallacht* on him—a general and comprehensive curse.

The *slua-mhallacht* seems to have neither frightened nor tamed MacGrath. On the next Sunday after the malediction, he arrived in the little church in Tooraneena, strode up to the altar and began to beat the priest. So terrified were the local people of both the attacker and all the *Clanna Buí* that none dared defend the priest except a stranger who managed to separate the two. This incident, of course, constituted a sacrilege and the bishop decided to investigate the matter. The result of this episcopal visitation was that the poor priest was condemned for uttering the curse and MacGrath supported. Furthermore, to punish the curser, his bishop decreed that each Sunday henceforth he should go the long distance to Dungarvan to say Mass in the morning and then come back to do the same in Tooraneena.

Eventually the priest was delayed one Sunday by wind and rain and he arrived after midday from Dungarvan. According to regulations he dare not say Mass at this time. He went to the church where the congregation was waiting patiently and said:

As to those who are guilty of all this, the world will see that they won't have a day's luck and will disappear like the froth of the river!

It is said that the killer died within a week of this final malediction. Local tradition states that when his remains were being carried across the fields to Knockboy cemetery, the priest who had cursed him saw someone replacing a gap-closing which had been opened to allow the funeral through. 'Leave it open!' said he, 'There are more of them to come!' Within a year all the males of that generation of the *Clanna Buí* died and were buried in Knockboy, or so tradition tells us.

The main facts of the above story are substantially true and one must decide whether the series of incidents which led to the deaths of half-a-dozen men of the same family was coincidence or the result of malediction.

Sectarianism

There is a story from the North of Ireland of an

incident which took place in the last century and which drew down a priest's curse on the leading character in the story. The type of incident described is all too common nowadays but was not unknown in the past.

A priest had installed a new door in his house and had a glass panel placed above it on which a chalice had been depicted. This did not please some of the local Protestants. One night some of them were drinking in a public house belonging to a co-religionist and when they left the place, they went to the presbytery armed and led by the publican. There a shot was fired through the glass panel but nobody was injured. Any type of legal redress was out of the question in that type of society and so the priest cursed whoever fired the shot, saying, 'The arm that fired that shot is not known, but it will be known before this day week!' The malediction was pronounced publicly from the altar of the church.

It is said that the public house, where the incident was planned, was sold a week afterwards! Furthermore, it is said that the publican became insane and had to be confined in the mental home where he made constant efforts to eat his right arm and hand. Everyone was then convinced that he was the sniper who had fired into the priest's house.[2]

Another story with a sectarian colouring is told in the Clogheen district in south-west Tipperary. A family, called Perry, were landlords here since after the time of Cromwell and their reputation was rather bad. For example, one of them is said to have incurred the curse which followed the execution of Father Sheehy in 1766, because a Perry had been on the jury which wrongly convicted the priest. Part of that curse was that the dwelling of the Perrys would be inhabited by crows. When 1921 came around and this part of the malediction had not yet been fulfilled, some local IRA men burned down the house and told the Perry of the time that naturally he was a nice fellow but that the old curse must be fulfilled! At some time during the last century a Perry decided to greet the appointment of a new Parish Priest with

68

a public insult. He forced his Catholic workmen to labour on a holiday of obligation opposite the church. The priest reacted with fury when he noticed this and also the fact that Perry himself was there to enjoy the priest's reaction. He was quite unprepared for what he heard. 'Perry', said the priest, 'if you don't release these men for Mass at once, I'll lay a mark on your soul that you'll never remove!' This, we hear, had the desired effect.

The O'Flaherty Curse

The O'Flahertys were a powerful family in County Galway in the past but eventually just one of the name was left with land and property. When this man died, it was said that he had been the object of a priest's curse.

It is said that O'Flaherty evicted a widow who had a son who was a priest. Not satisfied with evicting her, he also had her two last sheep sheared, although it was in the winter. Consequently they died of exposure. This action drew on him the malediction of her son, the priest, who reached beyond the grave with his punishment. He said that O'Flaherty would die and that his ghost would walk restlessly for ever by the lake-shore near the old family-home.

Tradition says that O'Flaherty died a month after the utterance of the curse and people in the area claimed to have seen his ghost on the lake-shore, pacing back and forth, his legs as thin as the shanks of sheep. Not only did he die, but all his relatives followed soon afterwards in a mass exodus of the O'Flaherty clan to the after-life. All this was attributed to the priest's curse.[3]

Medieval Sacerdotal Curses

In the Irish annals there are some examples of curses put on people by clerics and they are invariably reactions to some kind of military tyranny carried out by the English or their Irish agents. The cynic will observe that if the clerical curse was that effective, why on earth did our ancestors ever use force of

arms to defend themselves instead of hiring out a goodly number of sacerdotal cursers to serve their purpose.

The Annals of the Four Masters, or to give them their proper title, *The Annals of the Kingdom of Ireland,* mention under the date A.D. 1188 the death of one Donal O'Cananain. This fellow had injured his foot accidentally with an axe and probably died of septicaemia. The annals point out, however, that he died as the result of the curse of Colm Cille put on him by the priests of Derry. God alone knows what deeds brought down this curse on the fellow.

There is another story from the same annals which centre around the Battle of Moylurg in A.D. 1233. In that battle one Felim O'Connor of Connacht defeated a mixed force of O'Connor relatives and non-Irish. Since the death of Rory O'Connor, the last King of Ireland, his people had been engaged in internecine warfare in which the English authorities interfered and always to the detriment of the older inhabitants of the island. At the Battle of Moylurg the leader of the defeated O'Connors was Aodh Muimhneach and the annalists give the following explanation for his death: The church of Tibohine in County Roscommon had been wrecked and plundered some time before by Aodh Muimhneach and his friends. It is reported that the clergy of Connacht cursed them 'with bell, book, crozier and extinguishing of candles' i.e. by the official curse of the Church. According to the annals this was the cause of the defeat of these men and their army at Moylurg in 1233.

Motives : Serious and Frivolous

The motives for sacerdotal maledictions mentioned so far are social injustice, murder, violence to a priest or desecration of a church. If cursing be considered a justifiable practice, then one must admit that these motives may constitute full and sufficient reason for it. In folklore-stories one often finds some odd and interesting motives for priestly curses.

For example, in July 1947 the All-Ireland Semi-Final hurling match between Galway and Kilkenny was played in Birr. After an extraordinarily tense and exciting game the Galway team was leading by two points a few moments before the end. Then suddenly the score was equalised and just before the referee blew the final whistle Kilkenny scored a winning point. Naturally this was a bitter disappointment to the Galway people and some of them were convinced that this was the result of a priest's curse! It appears that on the morning of the game a large number of men left the church in Galway before the Mass was quite finished and the Parish Priest was quite angry. He warned the departing fellows, 'You will be always within a point of it and you will never win it!'[4]

A rather peculiar story is recorded from Kilworth in County Cork. It is said that the people of this district in Gaelic-speaking times never cared for the beautiful old song, *Cailín deas crúite na mbó* (Pretty Girl Milking her cow). The reason was alleged to be a priest's curse. It was said that one night a priest was called to the bedside of a dying man and had to make a rather long journey. On the way he heard this song being sung so beautifully inside a fence and he stopped to listen to it. He was naturally very curious about the identity of the singer and he climbed over the fence to see for himself. What he saw on the far side of the fence was a great black dog. He understood that this was the devil who wished to delay him on his errand. The priest hurried off and when he reached the end of his journey, he found that the sick man had died. The priest then solemnly cursed the song and it is said that the people in the Kilworth area never liked it afterwards. One wonders what the truth of the dislike of this song was because this story appears to be a 'rationalisation', if that be the correct term in such a case![5]

In the Carrick-on-Suir area there was a story told about one of the Lord Waterfords who was under the curse described in Chapter II above. It is said that Lord Waterford met a priest whose name was Spratt and he twitted him about his name. Father Spratt

72

was rather short in humour and he retorted viciously, 'You will go and live always in that place where the fishes and sprats live!' The man who was addressed was drowned at sea afterwards, the subject, they say, of a double curse!

In olden times the most pathetic types of wanderers and outcasts in the Irish countryside were probably the 'broken priests'—those suspended from the exercise of their priestly functions by their bishop. They were brutally deprived of a means of livelihood and were unemployed and unemployable, going about ragged and destitute, depending for sustenance on the charity of the people. The curse of a suspended priest was especially feared. There is one story which comes to mind about one such man who visited a house not far from Clonmel. When the lady of the house saw the poor fellow in the distance, she instructed her servant-girl to inform him that she was not at home. When the suspended priest heard this, he remarked, 'She won't be here any other time I'll call!' It is said that the lady died soon afterwards and that this was due to the curse of the broken priest.

. . . . . .

The stories one hears of the priest's curse seem rather like the kind of anecdote which attaches itself to someone who is held in superstitious dread. In the novels of the nineteenth century based on Irish life, the priest appears as a good-hearted, fatherly leader of a flock of peasants, what is known as 'the Soggarth Aroon'. That this was partly true, one does not deny, but there were other dimensions to the matter. One of these was the maledictory powers which people attributed to priests. One remembers being somewhat shocked to hear a middle-aged general practitioner in a country town say seriously, 'Keep in with the priests! It is not lucky to fall out with them!' One also remembers the old saying from an area in the south-east of Slievenamon concerning priests, which refers to their occult powers, 'Keep out from them, if you want to keep in with them!'

NOTES

1. Folklore Ms 84 p 221
2. Folklore Ms 815 pp 136-7
3. Folklore Ms 90 pp 10-11
4. See *Irish Times* 17 January, 1974 (Article by Breandán Ó h-Eithir—'An Chaint sa tSráidbhaile'.)
5. Folklore Ms 54 p 47

CHAPTER VI

THE POET'S CURSE

The position of the poet in ancient Ireland and even up to the present day has always been honourable and often surrounded with mystical significance. It is evident from the annals that poets were believed to be capable of cursing and, although the records of Pre-Christian times are especially rather suspect as to their veracity, they preserve an attitude which has been found true in later days. For this reason much of the material preserved in what must be pseudo-history is worth considering.

The Glám Dícenn

The rituals connected with the *glám dícenn* have already been noticed in this work and they seem to prove that this was really a cursing ritual. Some stories in the legendary or semi-legendary early stories of Ireland would seem to bear this out.

There is one interesting example mentioned of the *glám dícenn* being used to influence the result of a battle. This concerns the Battle of Moytura, which is alleged to have taken place in the west of Ireland between people known as Tuatha Dé Danann (pro-bably euhemerised deities) and the Fomorians. Before the battle takes place, the leader of the Tuatha Dé Danann, Lug, asks the poet, Cairpre, what powers he could wield in battle. He replies that he can make a *glám dícenn* on enemies so that they could not resist warriors! He thereupon utters a *glám dícenn* on the foes and they are defeated.[1]

The poet Aithirne is supposed to have lived at some time about the beginning of the Christian era. He had two sons who became interested in the wife of Conor

MacNessa, the King of Ulster. It is said that when they made advances towards her, she resisted them and they composed a *glám dícenn* on her which disfigured her face with three blisters. One of these was white, another was red and the third was black. So humiliated was she that she died of shame. When Conor discovered the cause of her death, he raided the dwelling place of the malefactors and put them to death. One is led to speculate as to whether this was actually possible. It could be true that severe trauma could have caused blisters and this lends a semblance of truth to what might appear at first glance merely a naive legend from olden times.[2]

More celebrated than the story of Aithirne's sons is that of Caeir who was supposedly a king in Connacht in Pre-Christian times. Caeir was unfortunate in three things: He had a dissatisfied wife, a nephew in whom his wife was interested, and a knife which he was under strict *geis,* or taboo not to part with. The queen decided to rid herself of her husband and she knew that the infliction of a physical blemish on him would accomplish this, because this disqualified a man from kingship under the old Gaelic laws.

It was considered a serious breach of courtesy and an even more serious loss of face for a ruler to refuse a poet the fee he demanded in ancient Ireland. The queen prevailed on her husband's nephew, Néde, to demand the knife as a reward for a poem, knowing that her husband could not possibly solve the dilemma he found himself in. When Caeir found himself trapped by the nature of Néde's request, he was effectively destroyed. Néde was obliged to compose a *glám dícenn* on him which was as follows:

> *Maile baire gaire Caieur!*
> *combeodutar celtra catha Caeir!*
> *Caeir diba Caeir dira Caeir foro!*
> *fomara fochara Caeir!*

This quatrain is rather obscure but may be translated as follows:

> Evil, death, short life to Caeir;
> May spears of battle destroy Caeir!

May Caeir perish! may Caeir pay! may it reach Caeir!
Under rocks and mounds may Caeir be! [3]

What ritual accompanied this malediction is not recorded but three blisters arose on the king's face—red, white and black—which so disfigured him that he fled in shame, leaving both wife and kingdom to Néde. There the story might have concluded had Néde not repented of his conduct in laying a curse on an innocent man. He decided to visit Caeir in his refuge and journeyed in the former king's chariot accompanied by the origin of all the bother—the queen. When they reached Caeir's hiding-place, Néde insisted on coming face to face with him. Caeir died instantly of shame and at the moment of his death a rock nearby exploded, sending a splinter into Néde's eye and killing him at the same moment. It is extremely interesting to notice the part that a stone plays in the conclusion of this story. The part which stones played in maledictory practices is quite remarkable. In this case the stone was the instrument which punished the unjust curser. However it should be noted that the poet in this story, as well as in that concerning the sons of Aithirne, had the power to curse unjustly, although an enraged husband punished the sons in one case and Nature itself caused the very stone to burst with indignation in the other case and kill the unjust man.

The Convention of Druim Ceat has already been mentioned, where Colm Cille is said to have defended the poets against expulsion from Ireland. One of the complaints against them was their custom of charging exorbitant fees and then satirising those who could not pay them. It seems almost certain that the use of the *glám dícenn* was surely feared and the control of situations like that of Caeir and Néde was desired. The poets or *filid* of ancient Ireland were more than mere rhymers or poets, as we understand the term today. They were regarded as seers and as people with supernatural powers. It occurs to one that their cursing habits may have been taken over to some extent by the Christian establishment, which partly replaced them.

One should refer briefly to a satirical work which made fun of the ancient poets' powers of extreme satire, in other words, cursing. It tells of the early Christian days when the poet, Senchán Torpéist, exercised his powers by rhyming rats to death! [4] This is an interesting Irish twist on what one might call a Gaelic Pied Piper motif!

Medieval Gaelic Poets

Although the poets' powers were curtailed to some extent by Christianity, they still remained honoured and feared members of society. They survived the Norman Invasion because all Ireland was not subjugated and later the descendants of the invaders adopted Gaelic ways and supported the literary men, especially the 'bards', as the *filid* are often erroneously described. It should be noticed that a bard was really an inferior type of poet; a mere rhymer and not to be confused with the *filid* or poets, properly so called.

In many of the poems from the Middle Ages a malediction appears. For example, in a love-song the poet bursts out with *Mo mhallacht ort, gibé thú/ a fhir thuigeas run mo rann,/ Má chreidir go h-éag do mhnaoi* . . . (My curse on you, whoever you are,/ Oh man who knows my poem's riddle,/ If ever you trust a woman . . .). One wonders just how seriously this was intended or whether it was a form of emphatic statement. [5]

The annals record the coming of John Stanley to Ireland as viceroy in 1443 and note that he gave neither sanctuary nor mercy to clerics or literary men. When he died within a year, it was widely believed that his death had come about through the malediction laid on him by a poet. The poet in this case was one Niall O'Higgins of the present County Westmeath, whose property Stanley had despoiled and whose goods he had robbed in a foray. It is said that one Henry Dalton robbed one of the king's people in return, made restitution to O'Higgins out of the loot and finally escorted him into Connacht where he was safe across the Shannon from Stanley. Here Niall O'Higgins 'satirised' Stanley and when he died, it was considered a result of this curse.

At this point it should be emphasised that there were many types of satire known to Gaelic poets but that the opinion of the present writer is that one of them at least, the *glám dícenn,* appears to have been formal cursing. Whenever, therefore, one reads that a poet 'satirised' someone, it could vary from mockery and sly abuse to a fearful malediction. We are not concerned here with the ordinary satire known to Gaelic and English literature.

Later Gaelic Poets

In the seventeenth century the Gaelic system was finally destroyed and the poets suffered the fate of the conquered. Henceforth they were without wealthy patrons and became peasant-poets, poor wanderers depending on the old respect which a poet always had earned in Ireland. The memory of former times and the prestige which had been theirs in the past expresses itself sometimes in bitter verse and occasionally in maledictions.

The poet, Peadar Ó Doirín, lived from 1704 until 1764 in Ulster. He appears to have been disappointed in love and he vented his rage and frustration in the poem known as *An Guairne* which is full of venom. In translation here is a particularly vicious stanza:

May hound-wounding, heart-ache, and vultures gouging her eyes,
Derangement and madness on her mind come soon!
May the entrails and mansion of pleasure out of this worm fall out!
But may she still be alive till everyone's sick at the sight!

Having relieved himself thus far of his rage, Ó Doirín goes on:

81

Rain and fire; illwind and snow and hard-frost follow
her!
May Aeolus chase her into the harbours of Acheron
down!
Nine times sicker than the Ulstermen's illness let
her be!
May this insect get an illness that Hippocrates
cannot cure! [6]

This series of maledictions must have been seriously
intended. It is sometimes urged that the poet's curse
in the times under consideration was never serious but
a joke, or at most a mere formula of abuse. No one
can contend that the above verses are jocular and they
do not sound like mere formula.

There is a story from County Kerry which illustrates
how seriously the poet's curse could be accepted. The
land around Lough Lene, near Killarney, had come
into the possession of one Minor Herbert. He decided
to defy the old taboo against sailing on Lough Lene
and when he was preparing to launch a boat, watched
by his tenants, the poet Seán Crón came by. Someone told Herbert that Seán Crón would write a poem
against him and Herbert threatened to hang him if he
did. In spite of this, Crón did so and he wished ill-
luck on Herbert's voyage and drowning to him:
*Ceann urraidh na loinge a bheith in íochtar,/Agus an
chuid eile desa daoine theacht saor.* (The boss of the
ship underneath/And the rest of the people being
saved.) This had a most unforeseen result. In full view
of everyone, the ship sunk and the crew were drowned
but Herbert survived. Crón fled for his life and lived
for years disguised as a woman to escape the wrath
of Minor Herbert.[7]

One of the most famous Kerry poets of the
eighteenth century was Eoghan Rua Ó Súilleabháin,
who was schoolmaster, poet, libertine and press-ganged
naval rating in his life. His verse vibrates with word-
music and merriment but he was roused to write a
cursing satire once when a woman who was repairing
his stockings before he went dancing refused to return
them until he had paid her. There are twelve stanzas

in the poem but this one should suffice to illustrate the kind of poem it is:

May the curse of curses in sorrow prostrate you now!
Scorn, disgrace, malediction by churches and bells!
Your old frame dead and lifeless with never a stir!
With none to wake your corpse; your limbs without a shroud! [8]

The poems preserved of the work of the Corkman, Seán na Raithíneach Ó Murchú (Seán Murphy) contain some interesting cursing poems. He wrote one such poem on the death of a bailiff in Cork city in 1737. He calls down hosts of demons, dragons and insects to torment and burn the dead man, Guinan, who was from Mallow. If poor Guinan was the oppressor which the poet asserted he was, then this was an occasion worthy of his cursing prowess. However, the most interesting example of a poet's curse written by Seán na Raithíneach was directed against someone who stole a sheep belonging to him! Not only did he write a comprehensive cursing poem—*a slua-mhallacht*—but he also invited other poets to contribute their share to the maledictory poem. He begins by wishing on the thief *Siolán 'is croch ard lá gaoithe amuigh*—'A noose and a high gibbet on a windy day outside'. He dwells with ferocious zest on the details of the hanging that he wishes on this fellow:

Téad righin chrochaitheach bhrostaitheach oiriúnach
Faoi chaolscrogall an chrochaire bhithiúnaigh
('A stiff hanging hasty suitable rope/Round the thin throttel of this thieving villain').

He then wishes that he may have no son who will give him anything in his day of need and goes on to hope that putrid flesh may be his lot for a year together with a great desire for it. Having disposed of all this matter, he threatened the cursing psalm on the thief and calls on the devils to torment him for

ever. Finally the poet curses those who ate any morsel of the stolen sheep, concluding with the words:

Céasadh 'is crochadh 'is crothadh 'is crith le corda!
('Torturing and hanging and shaking and trembling on a rope').

Having finished the principal malediction three poets add their confirmatory maledictions. Seán Builléad from Cork issues a general curse, Eamonn de bhFál from Dungourney wishes the plague and eternal damnation to him, while Marcus Lee, a Protestant from Carrignavar, specifically sends him to hell. As he puts it:

Am molt ó ghoidis, a scriosaire an éithigh,
Thíos in ifreann guím thú 'ot chéasadh—
In íochtar an choire agus Oscar á shéideadh,
'Is deamhan 'is fiche acu 'ot ghiobadh as a chéile.
(Since you stole the sheep, you lying spoiler!
Into hell I wish you to be tormented—
In the depths of the whirlpool with Oscar blowing
(i.e. the fire)
And twenty-one demons each tearing you asunder.)

This is a good example of the *slua-mhallacht* and who wonders whether it was all an elaborate joke or else over-reaction on the part of the poet.[9]

The old Latin saying *De mortuis nil nisi bonum* ('Of the dead, tell only what is good') is scarcely true where one small poem by the Connacht blind songster, Anthony Raftery, is concerned. He lived in Connacht in the nineteenth century and it is said that he was treated meanly by the housekeeper of Frank Taafe in Killeadan, County Mayo. When he returned to Taafe's after her death, he asked to be led to her grave and instead of kneeling to pray, he uttered a curse which is as follows in translation:

I call on you, oh stone,
To keep Breed below.
She kept us short of drink
And on our house brought shame.
And since, oh Breed, you're buried now,
Eternal thirst to you and drought.[10]

Doneraile is a little village in north Cork which is more noted for its rural peace and the fame which the novelist, Canon Sheehan, brought it than for a cursing poem which is connected with it. It was written by Patrick Kelly whose watch was stolen while he was on a visit to the village. As the text suggests, Kelly suspected the local butcher of the theft. It has been suggested that Kelly was also vexed by the fact that a fulsome poem had been written by a barber named Edmund Holland, entitled 'On the Beautiful Seat of the Rt Hon Doneraile'. Kelly decided that he would inform the world at large that Doneraile had another side to its corporative character and so he set to work. He begins:

Alas! how dismal is my tale!
I lost my watch in Doneraile;
My Dublin watch, my chain and seal,
Pilfered at once in Doneraile.
May fire and brimstone never fail
To fall in showers on Doneraile!
May all the thieving fiends assail
The thieving town of Doneraile!

Further on Kelly refers to the suspected thief when he declares:

May beef or lamb or veal,
Be never seen in Doneraile!

This outspoken song was soon being sung far and wide to the annoyance of the Doneraile people. It is said that Lady Doneraile heard it and sent Kelly a new watch as a present and it is believed that he then composed a 'blessing poem' on the town. This, however, has not been preserved. It never could recover the ground lost to Doneraile by the cursing poem.[11]

The Doneraile song may be rightly regarded as just abuse in the form of a curse and not at all in the class of some of the Gaelic poems quoted above. Above all, it is totally distinct from the fearful *glám dícenn*. Besides, the nineteenth century poets were no

86

longer the powerful folk they had been earlier. Furthermore, whatever prestige and power they had in a Gaelic-speaking community still, was largely lost when people turned to the English language in an area and threw away much of the old culture.

Reminiscent of the Doneraile curse is one composed about Abbeyside, a part of Dungarvan in County Waterford. Abbeyside is on the north side of the little river which enters the sea at Dungarvan and was always patronisingly referred to by townspeople as 'the village'. At any rate a blind beggar visited Dungarvan and was robbed of his bag in Abbeyside. Unfortunately for the reputation of the area, the beggar was also a rhymer and ballad-writer and here is a portion of his thoughts on the people among whom he was robbed:

My curse attend Dungarvan,
Her boats, her borough and her fish!
May every woe that mars man,
Come dancing down upon her dish!
For all the thieves behind you,
From Slaney's banks to Shannon side,
Are poor scholars, mind you!
To the rogues you'd meet in Abbeyside.[12]

NOTES

1. See *Revue Celtique* iii where the Second Battle of Moytura is edited by Whitley Stokes, 1891, pp 91-102

2. 'The Wooing of Aithirne and the Death of Aithirne Here'—published in *Revue Celtique* xxiv by Whitley Stokes, 1903

3. *Three Irish Glossaries* London 1862 ed by Whitley Stokes p 24. The translation of the third line of the quatrain owes much to some suggestions offered by Professor Gearóid Mac Eoin of University College, Galway

4. See *Proceedings of the Royal Irish Academy* V pp 356-366

longer the powerful folk they had been earlier. Furthermore, whatever prestige and power they had in a Gaelic-speaking community still, was largely lost when people turned to the English language in an area and threw away much of the old culture.

Reminiscent of the Doneraile curse is one composed about Abbeyside, a part of Dungarvan in County Waterford. Abbeyside is on the north side of the little river which enters the sea at Dungarvan and was always patronisingly referred to by townspeople as 'the village'. At any rate a blind beggar visited Dungarvan and was robbed of his bag in Abbeyside. Unfortunately for the reputation of the area, the beggar was also a rhymer and ballad-writer and here is a portion of his thoughts on the people among whom he was robbed:

> My curse attend Dungarvan,
> Her boats, her borough and her fish!
> May every woe that mars man,
> Come dancing down upon her dish!
> For all the thieves behind you,
> From Slaney's banks to Shannon side,
> Are poor scholars, mind you!
> To the rogues you'd meet in Abbeyside.[12]

NOTES

1. See *Revue Celtique* iii where the Second Battle of Moytura is edited by Whitley Stokes, 1891, pp 91-102

2. 'The Wooing of Aithirne and the Death of Aithirne Here'—published in *Revue Celtique* xxiv by Whitley Stokes, 1903

3. *Three Irish Glossaries* London 1862 ed by Whitley Stokes p 24. The translation of the third line of the quatrain owes much to some suggestions offered by Professor Gearóid Mac Eoin of University College, Galway

4. See *Proceedings of the Royal Irish Academy* V pp 356-366

Chapter VII

THE WIDOW'S CURSE

The curse of the widow is probably the most celebrated curse of all. In bygone days, when women were less independent than they are nowadays and the state took no interest in their welfare (or in anyone else's for that matter), the lot of the widow could be sorrow and injustice. Often her only redress was to curse her oppressor with all her wide range of emotion intensified by frustration, rage and a sense of being unjustly treated. This, together with the fear of womanhood which is not far below the surface in primitive or rural societies, seems to have made the widow's curse feared.

One hears, for example, of a widow being evicted by a middle-aged bachelor farmer who acts legally but with scant respect for social justice. As he and his workmen throw out her bits of ramshackle furniture into the little yard, she solemnly curses him, saying: 'May you never be the father of a child that is your own!' Whatever the reason may be, whether that the curse really caused it or not, this man then marries and remains without an heir, while his many love-affairs embarrass him with their fertility.

Many people still speak of the widow's curse, although the actual cases one hears of are not as numerous as references to the maledictory practice would lead one to expect. One hears that widows cursing loosened their hair and often knelt while they uttered the imprecation. It must have been a chilling and impressive sight.

The Well

An old story relates that a landlord in the Kiltartan

area of County Galway, whose name was Niland, closed up a well on his property from which the women of the area drew water. This well had been used from time immemorial. If anyone nowadays attempted to do something like this, he would soon find himself in serious difficulties in the law-courts. In those times, however, no one would dare defy a landlord, who had immense powers over his tenants in practice if not strictly according to the law.

In spite of the closing of the area where the well was to trespassers, a poor widow entered the prohibited area to draw water from the well as she had always done. Niland met her and beat her severely. She went down on her knees, loosened her hair and solemnly cursed him. It is not recorded what words she used but it is said that from that day onwards he became progressively lame and became quite crippled before his death.[1]

Notice in this story the motive of the malediction, which was violence to a widow, and the ultimate cause of the curse was a crime against women because drawing water was always traditionally 'women's work'.

The Widow's Son

The theme of the hanging of a widow's son and the subsequent curse being laid on the guilty party is quite common all over Ireland. One interesting example of this comes from Drimoleague in West Cork.

It seems that a raid for arms was carried out on the house of one Gilman, a landlord. The raider was called Ó Duibhlios, a widow's son, who bungled the raid and was captured. For this deed Gilman had the young fellow hanged as an example to others. His widowed mother composed a lament for him in which she included a curse, as follows:

A Ghilman chiardhubh, díth agus cás ort!
Go maraí do chapall ar bholg na páirce tú!
Mar gheall ar an ní úd do bhi síleach gháidleah—

Cúpla gunna dá gcaithtí thar phál iad.
(Harm and death to you, swarthy Gilman!
In the middle of the field may your horse kill you!
Because of what was small and worthless—
A pair of guns, though o'er a fence thrown.)[2]

The preceding story belongs to the period before the 1798 troubles in Ireland when such arms-raids were rather common and such harsh punishments as hanging were quite common also. The next story involving the curse of a widow after her son's death is from Inistioge in County Kilkenny and it is alleged to have taken place before the Jacobite War in Ireland which began in 1689.

Near Inistioge one can still see the ruins of Brownsford Castle which formerly belonged to a family of FitzGeralds. The last FitzGerald to live there was known as 'the Baron'. Tradition states that one of his tenants, a widow, had some problems trying to keep her only son under control and she complained him to the 'Baron'. FitzGerald unwisely heeded her and remarked grimly: 'He'll be quiet from now on!' He then took the young fellow and beat him so badly that he killed him. This drew on the 'Baron' the curse of the bereaved widow who called down misfortune on the killer and said that the four winds of heaven would blow through his castle in Brownsford. It is an historical fact that this FitzGerald was a casualty at the Battle of Aughrim in 1691. It is also a fact that Brownsford Castle was forsaken and that its walls stood naked under the skies. This, it was said, was the result of a widow's curse.[3]

The Dagger-Woman

A much more colourful character by far than the 'Baron' was Nuala Burke, nicknamed *Nuala na Mideoige*—Nuala of the Dagger. This ferocious person is the subject of an interesting story from the Williamstown area on the borders of Counties Roscommon and Galway.

The Burkes were descended from the Norman de Burgo family who settled in Galway and Mayo in the

93

twelfth century. They became hibernicised to such a degree that the two main branches were known by Gaelic names—Mac Liam Uachtar and Mac Liam Íochtar. As the central power of the Dublin government increased by the seventeenth century, that of such families as the Burkes declined. Nuala of the Dagger was the last one of the many off-shoots of the Burkes.

She earned her nickname, it is said, by stabbing her twelve sons to death. Eventually she was left a widow and although she owned three castles, she spent the last of her days in an island castle called Corlough. So poor had she become that she used visit the mainland stealthily at night and steal food. She solemnly cursed, it is said, anyone who dared take even a stone from any of her castles for building—a custom which was not uncommon in Ireland. As a result of this unusual widow's curse, her castles were not interfered with and she was allowed to live her furtive existence, although her murders could have brought her to the gallows.

Nuala died when she visited a house on Hallowe'en and took some calcannon which had been left on the window-sill of a house for the spirits. The housewife had poisoned the food and this was the end of Nuala. She succeeded in dragging herself to her little boat and rowing out to the island-castle where she died. People whispered about the fact that the ferocious widow had the strength to dig her own grave under the castle-walls, which fell on the grave when she was dead and filled it! [4]

Lady Iveagh

Lady Iveagh, the husband of Colonel Thomas Butler of Kilcash in south Tipperary, was in striking contrast to Nuala of the Dagger. She was the widow of Lord Iveagh but was always known as 'Lady Veagh' by the tenants of her husband in the Kilcash area. Her husband had been a Jacobite and had also fought at Aughrim in 1691. After his death, years afterwards, Lady Veagh made the castle in Kilcash a refuge for Catholic clergy who were often fugitives from the law

94

of the land, due to the Penal Laws enacted against them.

The possibility that her husband's son and heir would conform to the Protestant religion was a cause of worry to her after her husband's death and it is said that she put a curse on him if he did so, stating that he would break his neck. According to an old tradition, this was the reason for his death when he fell from his horse on South Avenue in full view of the upper windows of the castle, where his mother witnessed his death. He had conformed to the rival faith some time before.[5]

It should be stated that this story is at variance with all the other stories which one hears about the gentle Lady Veagh. It illustrates how great the religious hates and the tensions engendered by sectarianism were at that time in Ireland.

·　·　·　·　·　·

These few examples of the widow's curse should illustrate what was believed in Ireland long ago. Occasionally one still hears some stories around this theme. One hears, for example, of some IRA men raiding a house in south Tipperary in 1921 to take the son of a widow for execution because it was understood that he had passed important information to the British authorities. Not only his mother, but also his sister confronted the armed men and they also shot her in their nervous reaction to her tirade of abuse. The mother solemnly cursed them. She said that the arm which fired the shot at the girl would rot on the man who killed her. Strangely enough the gunman died in great pain from some disease which affected his arm and the others who were there that night died afterwards in rather unpleasant and unusual ways. Was it all a coincidence?

NOTES

1. Folklore Commission Ms 538 p 390

2. Folklore Commission Ms 46 p 410
3. Folklore Commission Ms 94 p 60
4. Folklore Commission Ms 79 p 364
5. *Béaloideas* Vol VI p 185 Article by Pádraig Ó Milleadha

CHAPTER VIII

CURSING FORMULAE

In the Ireland of today probably the only remnant of cursing which is widespread is the use of cursing formulae. Indeed this is what people generally understand 'cursing' to be. The great distinction between genuine cursing and the use of 'curse-words' or cursing formulae is that in the former case evil is intended and in the latter case there is no such serious intention. One hears expressions which could be quite spine-chilling if meant seriously but which become harmless by use and the lack of strong motive.

In this chapter it is intended to give some examples of cursing formulae which either are in use or which are recorded by reliable reporters. It will be noticed that some of the most picturesque ones are those found in Gaelic, the language which may enshrine nearly two thousand years of the experience of the Irish people and which has remained quite close to the roots of the racial consciousness.

The Devil

It is correct to state that the 'devil' personifies the principle of evil and therefore it is no wonder to find expressive cursing formulae invoking him.

1. 'The devil sweep him!'

2. 'The devil swallow him sideways!'

3. *Th'anam 'on diabhal!* ('Your soul to the devil!')

This expression was often used and the author remembers an old Gaelic-speaking relative explaining laboriously that she had said: *Th'anam ón diabhal!* i.e. 'Your soul *from* the devil!' instead of the malediction!

99

4. *An diabhal go ndéana sé storc díot!* ('May the devil make a fool of you!') In this case *storc* is borrowed from the English 'stirk' which means a young heifer or a bullock and was used also in English as a term of abuse.

5. *Bheirim don diabhal sibh!* ('I give you to the devil!')

6. *Go mbainidh an diabhal an ceann díot agus obair lae ded mhuinéal!* ('May the devil cut the head off you and make a day's work of your neck!') This horrible reference to an inefficient headsman is rather chilling!

7. *Go ropa an diabhal thú!* ('May the devil tear you!')

8. 'May old Harry run away with him!' In this case the devil's name is disguised. Whether this is any reference to some diabolical tendencies which King Henry VIII may have been thought to have or not, is not clear.

9. 'Go to the dickens!' Here again the devil's name is under disguise.

10. *Th'anam 'on diucs!* ('Your soul to the dickens!') This curse uses a Gaelic form of 'dickens' for 'devil'.

11. *Go ndamnaí an diabhal síos go leac na corónach thú, nó go tobar na luaithe seacht míle taobh thíos d'ifreann; agus go mbrise an diabhal do chnámha! Mo chuid tubaiste agus anachain agus urchóid na bliana ort!* ('May the devil damn you to the stone of dirges, or to the well of ashes seven miles below hell; and may the devil break your bones! And all my calamity and harm and misfortune for a year on you!')[1]

This full-blooded curse comes from the Cois Fharraige area, west of Galway city in Connemara. It is rather comprehensive damning of someone to hell.

12. *In ifreann go rabhair mar gheall led' pheasaí!*
Ag an diabhal go riabh th'anam agus garda air!
Mar dhearbhaigh tú le feall gur ceann ar na craipís

An Paorach nach bhfuairis a cháineadh.
(In hell may you be because of your sins!
May the devil have your soul under guard
there!
For you treacherously swore that the head of
the croppies
Was Power whom you couldn't disparage.)[2]

This curse was pronounced against the betrayer of
Edmund Power, who was hanged in the Market Place
in Dungarvan in 1798. It forms part of an elegy for
Power and it should be noted that often a curse was
inserted in such cases where the death was a political
execution or had undertones of political or racial
injustice.

13. 'To hell with him'. This is a very common curse.

14. 'To Halifax with him!' Here the name of hell
is under disguise.

15. 'Hell roast him!'

16. 'May the devil roast the —— off him!' In the
space provided the user of this curse could insert some
part of the anatomy, especially a sexual organ.

17. The author remembers a cruelly abusive song
composed by a bitter old woman years ago against a
local man which ends thus:

And the day will come, when he'll be cold and
dumb,
And roast for eternity!

18. 'May the devil take him by the heels and shake
him!' This particular curse has a light-hearted ring
and does not have the bitterness of the others.

Misfortune

It is natural that the invocation of general ill-luck and
misfortune on another should form a part of curses
used. Here is a selection of them:

1. 'Bad luck to him!' This curse is used so much
that it seems to have lost its sting altogether.

101

2. 'Bad cess to him!' The word 'cess' was the term used in Ireland in the sixteenth century especially for money levied for the upkeep of military forces. The inference in the curse needs no further comment!

3. *Droch-rath air* ('Bad luck to him!')

4. *Cumhradh ar an airgead!* ('Confusion on the money!') This is a curse on a wealthy person.

5. *Bris chráite na bliana ort!* ('The anguished bankruptcy of the year to you!')

6. 'Sorra do him good with it!' ('May it do him no good, only sorrow!') This ill-wish is for the buyer of an article or some property.

7. 'May he never have a day's luck!' This is the usual form of a general curse found in the English language in Ireland today.

8. *Im ná raibh ar do bhainne, cliath ná raibh ar do lachain, siúl ná raibh ag do leanbh, agus feannadh ar do bhó. Is go mba mó 'is ba leithne an lasair, a bhéas ag dul trí d'anam, na sléibhte Chonamara, agus iad a bheith á ndó.* ('No butter be on your milk, nor on your ducks a web; may your child not walk and your cow be flayed! And may the flame be bigger and wider, which will go through your soul, than the Connemara mountains if they were on fire!') This extraordinary curse was pronounced by a blind man on a housewife when she had been less than generous with him![3]

Illness

The curses in Gaelic and in English seem to some extent to concentrate on sudden pains, respiratory troubles and the like. One is tempted to state that these kind of complaints can very easily be psychosomatic and induced by tension brought about by worry over a curse.

1. *Go lagaí Dia thú!* ('May God weaken you!')

2. *Tachtadh ort!* ('Choking to you!')

102

3. *Do thachtadh chugat !* ('May your choking come on you! ')

4. *Go mbuaile an arrainn thú!* ('May a stitch or convulsion strike you! ')

5. *Ciorrbhadh ort!* ('May you be mangled! ') The term *ciorrbhadh* may also mean being 'overlooked' by someone with the evil eye.

6. *Duig nimhe ionat!* ('A poisonous pain in you! ')

7. *Bás is múchadh ort!* ('Death and smothering on you! ')

8. *Fiabhras buinneach ort!* ('Dysentery on you! ')

Death

Since death was the final mortal misfortune which could be wished on a person, it follows naturally after curses which concern illness.

1. *Cat mara agus marbhfháisc uirthi!* ('The sea-cat and death-strangling to her! ') The sea-cat was a mysterious animal whose visit was an omen of illness, misfortune and death. Traditions concerning this animal are found in the North of Ireland.

2. *Bás na bpisín chugat!* ('The death of the kittens to you! ') This, of course, means simply 'drowning', the fate of so many unwanted kittens in Ireland.

3. 'May he die roaring! ' This ugly curse is heard still occasionally.

4. 'May he fester in his grave! '

5. 'I loathe and detest the miserable bastards! . . . May they rot in hell! ' This full-blooded curse comes from the pen of Lord Arran, who described the Irish people in this fashion in a newspaper column in May 1974.

6. *Bás gan sagart chuige i mbaile gan chléireach!* ('A death without a priest to him in a town without a clergyman! ') To an Irish Catholic, to whom execution was not a far-fetched notion in the past, this was a rather fearful curse, carrying with it the threat

103

of eternal damnation. It comes rather suitably after the preceding curse! It could be a suitable response to it.

7. *Nár fheice tú an chuach nó an traona!* ('May you not see the cuckoo nor the corncrake!') In other words, may you never see another spring!

8. *Mo mhallacht ort is léir ort, a rascail bhradaigh bhréagaigh,*
Nára fada an lá go n-éagfair gan bhuíochas Mhic Dé . . .

('My curse on you and ruin to you, you lying, thieving rascal!

Let it not be long till you die, despite the son of God! . . .')

This curse, inserted in the lament on a family of Connerys of Bohadoon in County Waterford, deals with the informer who had a hand in their transportation.[4]

9. *Íde coileach Éamoinn ort!* ('The fate of Ned's cock to you!') This is a reference to a cock who was so vain that he stood admiring himself in the water of a well and fell in and got drowned. This is a curse on a vain person!

General

Here follows an assortment of maledictions of various types.

1. *Maldacht a gaiscid fair!* ('The curse of his weapons upon him!') This is a wish that the cursed one will die in battle. It is one of the oldest curses extant in the Gaelic language.

2. *Maldacht na truagh ocus na trén ar an té do tug!* ('The curse of the wretched and the strong on the one who gave!')

3. 'Tattheration to him for a mule!' ('Destruction to that mule!')

4. 'Purshuing to them!' This curse arises of Irish history with its rebellions, raids and counter-raids.
104

Pursuit could generally have but one result—death.

5. *Guím diochair ar an tigh!* ('I pray for sorrow on the house!')

6. 'The curse of Jesus on you!' This curse has a companion where 'God' is substituted for 'Jesus'. It is worth noting that the Holy Ghost is never mentioned in this nor in any other cursing formula known to the author.

7. 'God damn him!'

8. 'God blast him!'

9. *Go n-ithig na cait na mná!* ('May the cats eat the women!') This misogyny was uttered by a beggar who was disappointed in his reception at a house where he sought food. He desires that the cats (household animals) may eat the women. He had been offered food which he considered fitter for a cat than a human being.

10. *Sionnach ar do dhubhán!* ('A fox on your fishing-hook!') Instead of fox, hare (giorria) or rabbit (coinín) might also be substituted. This was a Galway curse on a fisherman. For example, if a fisherman from the Claddagh saw a fox before he intended to go fishing, he went home without putting to sea. Foxes, hares and rabbits were regarded with superstitious dread by the fishermen of the Claddagh.

11. 'The curse of the crows on you!' This means 'May you never enjoy the fruits of your labours!' It was understood that the crows (as rooks are called in Ireland) worked for naught.

12. 'The curse of Cromwell on you!' This has been referred to already. It can also mean 'May you be afflicted with the itch and have no nails to scratch with!'

13. *Maidhm sléibhe anuas ort!* ('A mountain landslide down upon you!') This curse comes from the Glen of Aherlow in County Tipperary. Long ago the sides of the Galtee Mountains were notoriously unstable and led to destruction of houses and property when a landslide occurred in the Glen of Aherlow.

105

14. *Pé duine d'fhág mise faoi thuirse gan aird,*
   Is mo chat fireann bán go tláith uaim go deo;
   Go dtaga na lucha 'na dtulcái 'na dháil,
   Is francaigh na h-áithe go raibh ar a thóir.
   (Whoever put me into impotent grief
   And took my white tom-cat in secret from me,
   May the mice come in waves as his company,
   And the rats from the kiln give him the pursuit.)

This curse, composed by one James Kirwan of County Waterford, was uttered on the death of his tom-cat. It forms the last stanza of a lament with three stanzas.

15. *Mallacht na mbaintreach agus na ngalrach ort !*
('The curse of the widows and orphans on you!')

16. *Croch ard gaoithe chuige!* ('A high windy gallows to him!')

17. *Faoi shúiste Oscair go bhfaighe tú do charnadh !*
('May you garner under Oscar's flail!') Oscar was the strong man of the legendary Fianna and this curse means simply: 'May you earn what you can but under most difficult circumstances!'

18. *Cloch dhearg id scornaigh!* ('A red stone in your throat!')

19. 'May he melt away like the froth of the river!' This curse was quite common all over Ireland long ago.

20. *Gráin éisc !* ('Fishes' hate!') If this were shouted after someone going fishing, he was sure to return from the expedition with an empty bag!

21. *Húrú, a mhinistéir, a thug do dhá phingin dom*
   Tar éis do leanbh a chaoineadh;
   Oidhe an linbh ar an gcuid eile acu,
   Siar go h-eireaball timpeall.
   (Horo, oh minister, who gave me twopence
   After keening your infant;
   May his death come on the rest of them,
   Down to very last one!)

This curse was uttered by a keening woman who was ill-paid by a Protestant minister for her services and who then cursed his surviving family.

22. *A Mháire Ní Dhúinléith, go n-imí díth ort!*
Páiste trasna ort agus nár bheire tú coíche é!
Nó má bheiris, nár chosúil le Críostaí é!
Caincín muice air agus gob caorach!
Caincín muice air a chartfadh an t-aoileach!
Ar eagla gur crochaire é a chrochfadh na
daoine!
(Oh Moll Dunlea, may harm overtake you!
A child be within you, for ever unborn!
Or if be born, may he not be like a Christian!
A pig's snout on him and the mouth of a sheep,
A beak of a duck that could dredge in the
sludge!
Lest he be a hangman that would hang the
people!)

Behind this bitter curse is the story of Father
Nicholas Sheehy (hanged 1766 in Clonmel) on whom
Moll Dunlea is said to have informed and sworn per-
jured evidence. The abhorrence in which her name
was held in the Déise country (County Waterford and
south Tipperary) is well illustrated in these lines which
were uttered by a keening woman after the priest's
hanging.

23. *Gach lá bíodh sé fliuch agaibh!* ('May every day
of it be wet for ye!') This is the curse of Saint Patrick
on the Fair of Clonmel, according to tradition—it
always seems to be wet!

24. *A Íosa, a Dhia dhílis, agus a Athair an Uain,*
A chíonn sinn i gcuibhreach agus i gceangal
róchrua,
Faoi mar a dheinis Críostaithe dínn ó Aoine go
maidin Dé Luain,
Dein díon dúinn agus díbir an ghraithin seo
uainn!
(Oh Jesus, dear God and Father of the Lamb!
Who sees us in fetters and in bondage so hard!
As you made us Christians between Friday and
Monday,
Protect us and banish this scum from us.)

This verse was composed by the poet, Eoghan Rua
Ó Súilleabháin. Some soldiers were billeted on the
108

people in a parish where the poet was and a satire by the poet did no good either! Then he asked the priest to utter the cursing psalm against the soldiers but the priest suggested that the poet compose this mild malediction above which was taught to the parishioners and which they repeated over a week-end. We are told that the soldiers withdrew on a Monday morning.

25. *Cuirim· do gheasa troma draíochta ort, aniar chois amhna, siar/chois amhna, i dtom neanta go dtite tú, na madrai allta go n-ithe tú, cos leat ar sliabh . . .* ('I bind you by grave injunctions of magic, back from the river, back to the river, may you fall in a nettle-patch, may savage dogs eat you, one foot on a mountain . . .') This maledictive type of formula was heard being used by children at play without any attempt at serious cursing. It is quite possible that it may represent an ancient formula whereby someone was ordered to do something or carry out some order under pain of being cursed.

26. *Ná raibh dea-rath ort agus croisim aris thú.* ('May you have no good luck and I recant the curse! ') This is a recanted curse-formula. The word *croisim* (literally 'I cross') is the term used in these cases. This may be due to the use of a crucifix to bless the curse away or it may simply mean that the curse was 'crossed' or thwarted.

.   .   .   .   .   .

One should compare the richness of expression in the Gaelic curses above with the poverty of expression so often evident in the English ones. This, of course, is not confined to curses but is true of the Irish mode of expression in the English language generally.

Reference should be made here to the lore of the tinkers, or the itinerants, as it is fashionable to describe them nowadays. The impression has been created, especially by the plays of John Millington Synge, that these people have some rich vein of tradition which is somehow more rewarding and more expressive than that found among, say, the settled folk of

109

the countryside. This seems to be a fallacy to the present author. Repeated efforts to tap this 'rich vein' has resulted in uncovering a poverty of expression and tradition which is startling when one remembers that these people have been immune from the levelling influences of modern schools and society.

One should also note that in modern Ireland curse-words, such as those listed above, are giving way to mere four-letter words, as they are coyly described, which are imported. One tends to hear a dull obscenity in expression where one would have found the situation otherwise years ago. It may sound blackly humorous to advocate a return to cursing formulae but the dullness which has succeeded them is appalling.

NOTES

The principal sources of the curse formulae listed above are as follows: Folklore Manuscripts in University College Dublin, Séamas Mac Doncha MA, PhD of Galway, Tomás Ó Móráin BA, PhC of Clonmel, Dineen's *Irish-English Dictionary* (Dublin 1927) and other sources which are noted below. Where the author has personal knowledge of the matter, no reference to source is given.

'The Devil': Nos 6 & 7 from S Mac Doncha; No 11 from *Béaloideas* IV p 137; No 12 from Folklore Ms 84 p 209

'Misfortune': No 5 S Mac Doncha; No 8 *Béaloideas* IV p 137

'Illness': Nos 1, 2, 3, 4 from S Mac Doncha; No 7 from Mrs S Mac Doncha

'Death'; No 1 from Folklore Ms 289 p 289; No 2 from *Irisleabhar na Gaedhilge* VII p 89; Nos 6 & 7 from S Mac Doncha; No 8 from Folklore Ms 84 p 242

'General': Nos 1 & 2 from *Contributions to a Dictionary of the Irish Language* (1939) arranged by Maud Joynt (under word *Maldacht*) p 51a; Nos 11, 12, 13, 23 from Tomás Ó Móráin; Nos 5, 14, 20, 21, 22,

24, from Folklore Ms 259 p 717, 84 p 234, 54 p 205, 259 p 682, 84 p 61, 147 p 275; Nos 16 & 26 from S Mac Doncha; No 17 from *Abhráin Atá Leagtha ar an Reachtuire* by Douglas Hyde Dublin 1893 p 290; Nos 3 & 4 from *Fireside Stories of Ireland,* 1870, by P Kennedy p 99 and 41 respectively; No 25 from *Imtheacht na Tromdháimhe,* 1857 (Transactions of the Ossianic Society Vol V p 107 Prof Connellan)

CONCLUSION

The first thing that will probably strike the reader is the primitive type of society in which much of the material in the foregoing chapters was preserved. 'Primitive' is the term used advisedly to describe a community which believed in magic and the possibility of invoking powers not generally deemed part of ordinary human potential. To very many people at the present time cursing is mere superstition, and harmful superstition at that.

The large variety of practices, rituals, formulae and beliefs associated with maledictive customs emphasise the fact that it was spontaneous. Each curser tended to act according to the circumstances in which he or she found himself or herself. It was pre-eminently a folk-custom with wide local variations. If one were to attempt to establish a basic form which cursing could take, one is driven to state vaguely that some words were uttered invoking evil on others, accompanied often by certain simple or elaborate ceremonies.

Among the variety of cursing ceremonies the only one which seems based on established ritual is that associated with the cursing stones. It seems that the basic form here was i), the custom of fasting before the cursing act, ii), carrying out the ritual, if not also the fasting, in some hallowed place, iii), turning the spherical stones anti-clockwise. The last element in this ritual seems to be of Pre-Christian origin and perhaps also the second one. It could be true to say that the first one arose out of the excommunication practices of the Christian Church. In the absence of any reliable evidence, the question remains open. When one considers how much the ritualistic practices of Christianity are indebted to the religions which preceded it, one thinks that cursing was an integral part of Pre-Christian practice. The old lives of the

Irish saints are surely as unreliable as the Irish history of the period but the general impression given in them is hardly inaccurate and must be taken seriously. Taking the cursing practices of the hagiographies and the existence of cursing stones on ancient monastic sites into account, one cannot say that the old writers were merely drawing on their fantastic imaginations all the time.

It cannot be denied that a very large number of the tales which one finds in folklore were probably fabrications. It is also evident that coincidence played a large part in the 'effectiveness' of cursing. However, one is often left wondering. For example, what is one to make of the celebrated curse on the Achill railway? This branch-line was built towards the end of the last century as an amenity in this depressed area but was abandoned before the Second World War. It was said that a curse was put on it, according to which the first and the last train to use the line would carry corpses. It happened that the first train did carry such a cargo. However one may dismiss this as coincidence or hindsight, the amazing thing is that when the railway had just been closed, a number of migratory labourers from the island were killed in a burning in Scotland and a train was run on the line, now officially closed, to carry home the corpses.

With regard to whether a curse can be effective, one should not forget that it is a form of prayer-petition. The Gaelic word *guíodóireacht,* which is in use in the Ring area in County Waterford, means both 'praying' and 'cursing'. There is a sarcastic saying regarding a person using curse-words there which goes: *Nach pras a thagann an ghuíodóireacht chuige!* ('Isn't it fluent he is at cursing-praying!') If one is to admit that prayer of petition is effective, then one must also say that cursing may be effective.

There are many odd references to cursing in folk-belief. There is, for example, the belief in the South of Ireland that if a visitor to a house in the countryside departs without drinking the cup of tea which is offered, he leaves his curse on the house by so doing. It was also believed in many parts of Ireland that one who entered a shop and failed to buy something, might leave a curse on the business by this action.

There is an anecdote from a certain area in Munster which illustrates that the fear of being cursed is not yet dead. About twelve years ago a Parish Priest demanded some funds from an angry parish committee. He was rather unpopular and, instead of being diplomatic and tactful, he attempted to bully the all-male audience, which led to very unpleasant scenes during which they 'insulted' him. When during the course of the next six years some of the principal protagonists or their close relatives all died violently, the story got about that the priest had cursed them privately! This, of course, he probably never did, but it illustrates how near the surface the belief in malediction is still.

There is a rather scatological German saying which says 'Fluchen ist der Stuhlgang der Seele'. This may be translated as 'Cursing is the bowel-evacuation of the soul!' This seems to refer to the use of curse-formulae to relieve frustration and to provide an outlet for rage which might express itself otherwise in physical violence. Compared to the people in the neighbouring island, Irishmen are notorious for the use of 'curse-words', a characteristic which possibly has much to do with the long foreign domination of the country and the general national frustration to which it gave rise.

It is generally regarded as bad taste to use any kind of 'strong language', as people sometimes describe the use of cursing formulae in a non-serious manner, in the presence of women. This is surely a desire to avoid doing violence to women, because cursing of every kind is a form of verbal violence. One often wonders whether it is also based on an atavistic fear of the power of women in such matters, if their anger is aroused. It should not be forgotten that, of all the curses, the widow's curse was the one most universally feared and is referred to often as being very powerful.

There are also beliefs concerning the evil which harming certain wild creatures can bring on one. One hears of the curse which a frog can put on one if he is caught by the mouth! In such a case, it is said, the violator of the little creature falls down. A child's folk-belief, heard by the author, asserts that no one should harm a hedgehog because it 'brings little apples to God!' If one does, the hedgehog will curse one. What form the punishment would take, has not been specified. There is the old saying addressed to hens who trespassed on the kitchen of a farmer's house: *Cosa gloine fúibh!* ('Glass legs to ye!'), a neat way of expressing the wish that they might break their legs!

It is the reader's privilege to decide what validity the views expressed in this work may have. An attempt has been made to explore a corner of Irish life which has received little attention until now. That this facet of Irish life is not without importance and significance is the opinion of the author.